Living LITERATURE

READING POETRY

Frank Myszor

Hodder & Stoughton

A MEMBER OF THE HODDER HEADLINE GROUP

Acknowledgements

With thanks to Jeremy Hughes for permission to use *Valentile* and for his personal comments on the poem.

For Florence

The author and publishers would like to thank the following for :

Copyright text:

p. 1, *Ghost Train*, Sean O'Brien, Oxford University Press 1995; p. 9, The *Independent on Sunday*, Marguerite Jones, 1998; p. 10, *Poetic Truth*, R. Skelton, Random House Group 1978; p. 11, *Valentile*, Jeremy Hughes; p. 16, *Guardian Weekend*, Martin Amis, 1993; pp. 19– 20, *The Reader's Companion to Twentieth Century Writers*, ed. P. Parker, Helicon 1995; pp. 22–23; pp. 23–24, *A Journey into Thomas Hardy's Poetry*, Joanna Cullen Brown, WH Allen 1989; p. 24, *Room* is taken from *Mean Time* by Carol Ann Duffy, published by Anvil Press Poetry in 1993; p. 25, Sean O'Brien, *The Deregulated Muse*, Bloodaxe Books, 1998; p. 26, *The Pleasure of Reading*, ed. Antonia Fraser, Bloomsbury 1992; p. 35, Gwen Harwood, *Selected Poems: A New Edition* (Halycon Press, 2001), p. 23; pp. 37–38, *Source and Analogues of Chaucer's Canterbury Tales*, Bryan and Dempster, in Helen Phillips, *An Introduction to the Canterbury Tales: Reading, Fiction and Context*, Macmillan 2000; p. 46, *Morning Work* and *After the Opera*, DH Lawrence, from *Selected Poems of DH Lawrence*, ed. Reeves, Laurence Pollinger Ltd, 1951; p. 47, Grace Nichols, *The Fat Black Women's Poems*, Virago 1984; pp. 48–49, Reproduced from *Feminism and Poetry*, by Jan Montefiore, Pandora Press, London, 1994; p. 54, The *Oxford Companion to English Literature*, edited by Margaret Drabble (6th edition, 2000) © Margaret Drabble and Oxford University Press, 2000; p. 54, *It was not Death, for I stood up*, Emily Dickinson; p. 55, Excerpt from *Ted Hughes: The Unaccommodated Universe* Copyright © 1980 by Ekbert Faas and reprinted with the permission of Black Sparrow Press; p. 56, *The Hollow Men*, TS Eliot, in *Collected Poems 1963*, Faber and Faber; pp. 58–59, Steven Lynn, *Texts and Contexts*, HarperCollins 1994; p. 60, *Digging*, Seamus Heaney, in *Death of a Naturalist*, reproduced with permission of Faber and Faber 1966; p. 61, *Seamus Heaney: Open Guides to Literature*, Ronald Tamplin, OUP 1989; p. 64, *Meaningless* Verse, Dr Roe, The *Week*, Oct 2000, originally in *The Times*; pp. 85–86, *Tennyson: The Critical Heritage*, ed. John Jump, Macmillan 1972; pp. 87–88, *To the Sea*, Phillip Larkin, in *High Windows*, reproduced with permission of Faber and Faber 1974; p. 88, Reading 1, Alan Gardiner, in *Philip Larkin: The Poems*, ed. Linda Cookson and Bryan Loughrey, Pearson Educational 1989; p. 88, Reading 2, Peter Hollindale, ibid.; p. 89, Gail Ashton, *Studying Chaucer*, Studymates Limited 2000; p. 90, Caroline Cole, *Literary Review*, Vol 11, No 1, Sept 2000; p. 90, From *The Nature of Narrative*, by Robert Scholes, © 1968 by Oxford University Press, Inc. Used by permission of Oxford University Press, Inc; p. 91, Blake Morrison, *Seamus Heaney* in Contemporary Poets Series, 1982; p. 91, Philip Mallett, *John Donne, Selected Poems*, Pearson Education 1999; pp. 94–95, Student's answer, Bilqess Khan, p. 95, Teacher's comment, Pam Fisher.

Orders: please contact Bookpoint Ltd, 130 Milton Park, Abingdon, Oxon OX14 4SB. Telephone: (44) 01235 827720, Fax: (44) 01235 400454. Lines are open from 9.00–6.00, Monday to Saturday, with a 24 hour message answering service. Email address: orders@bookpoint.co.uk

British Library Cataloguing in Publication Data
A catalogue record for this title is available from the British Library

ISBN 0 340 79954 4
Published by Hodder & Stoughton Educational Scotland
First published 2001

Impression number	10 9 8 7 6 5 4 3 2 1
Year	2007 2006 2005 2004 2003 2002 2001

Copyright © 2001 Frank Myszor

Cover photo from The Ronald Grant Archive
Typeset by Fakenham Photosetting Limited, Fakenham, Norfolk NR21 8NN
Printed in Great Britain for Hodder & Stoughton Educational, a division of Hodder Headline Plc, 338 Euston Road, London NW1 3BH by J. W. Arrowsmith Ltd, Bristol.

Contents

1 Introduction: Who said Poetry is Dead?

Towards the end of the year 2000 the *Radio Times* and the *Daily Express* ran the same headline: 'Water, water, everywhere ...'. One appeared at the top of an article on water and health, the other as a front page reaction to the floods that occurred that year. Both were quoting Coleridge's two hundred year old *The Rime of the Ancient Mariner*. These references to a classic poem in the mainstream media suggest that poetry is alive and kicking. After all, neither of the above publications is exactly high brow! So never assume that poetry is just clever stuff with words that has no connection with everyday life.

Poetry is sometimes used as a yardstick for all that is beautifully performed or put together, as when you watch a skilful football player and the phrase 'poetry in motion' comes to mind. In fact, Sean O'Brien, in his 1995 collection *Ghost Train*, refers to the ex-Manchester United player Eric Cantona like this:

This 'luxury' is why the game survives,
This poetry that steps outside the book.

This book is about poetry that is increasingly being asked to step outside the book to be seen in a variety of contexts: historical, social, feminist and so forth.

ACTIVITY 1

Key Skills: Communication – discussion, reading (presentation)

To get warmed up for thinking about poetry, consider the way that poetry has been published in recent years. If you go into any good bookshop you will find that there are now anthologies of poetry about love, about bereavement, collections to help you through the day, and collections that trace the history of the twentieth century.

Create your own mini anthology of poetry collected with a particular purpose in mind. Divide the work into three phases:

a In a small group brainstorm the kinds of anthologies that could be written (you might have a lot of fun with this by considering, for example, an anthology of poems that you would least like your mother to read).

b Research: by using libraries, school anthologies, the internet and bookshops, collect poems to fit your chosen title (say, six poems).

c Share one or two of the poems in your anthology by reading them aloud to a group.

Where does this book fit in?

This book is particularly relevant to two AS and A level assessment objectives:

AO4: Candidates should be able to articulate independent opinions and judgements, informed by different interpretations of literary texts by other readers.

AO5i: Candidates should be able to show understanding of the contexts in which literary texts are written and understood (+ **AO5ii**: and evaluate the significance of cultural, historical and other contextual influences on literary texts and study).

At AS level it is highly likely that you will be given a critic's opinion of a poem and be asked to respond to it, both by giving your opinions of the critic's view and by providing your own reading of the poetry in question. This book develops both of these aspects.

At A2 you will need to deal with critics in a more sophisticated way. This is also covered, especially in the last chapter.

Key Skills

The National Qualification in Key Skills requires all AS and A level students to take the following key skills: Application of Number, Communication and Information Technology.

English Literature is relevant to two of these: Communication and Information Technology.

The Communication Unit includes:

- Discussion
- Making a presentation
- Selecting and synthesising information (reading)
- Writing different kinds of texts.

The Information Technology Unit includes:

- Plan and use different sources to search for and select information
- Explore, develop and exchange information, and derive new information
- Present information, including text, numbers and images.

You can be credited with key skills through any of the A levels or AVCEs that you are studying. This book indicates when an activity is relevant to the key skills of Communication or Information Technology. Here is how this is shown in the text:

Key Skills: Communication – discussion

Discuss with a partner whether or not you would consider *La Belle Dame Sans Merci* to be a progressive or non-progressive text. In other words does it offer approval of the 'society' described in the above diagram or is it critical of it?

An introductory text such as this can only give a brief indication of how the activities relate to key skills. For more detailed information you will need to look at key skills documents. You may then need to make adjustments to the activity according to your needs.

What this book is not about

- Don't expect to read about the traditional nuts and bolts of poetry reading: definitions of alliteration, metaphor, etc
- Don't expect catalogues of types of rhythms and rhyme used in English poetry
- Don't expect a history of English poetry from Chaucer via Shakespeare and Wordsworth to Ted Hughes
- Don't expect answers that you can memorise and use in your exams.

So, what are you getting?

- Advice about alternative ways of reading and writing about poetry
- How to use the readings of others to help your own
- How to write about poetry in various contexts
- Worked examples of analyses of a wide range of poetry from various periods.

How this book is organised

This chapter establishes ideas that will be used throughout the book:

- The idea of engaged reflection as a method of reading
- How poetry defies complete explanations so that uncertainty is inevitable
- Effective response to poetry is based on asking good questions – good questions cannot be easily answered
- How poetry can be read in different ways to produce different interpretations.

Thus, the present chapter emphasises alternative readings. Each chapter then explores the following ways of interpreting poetry: biographical criticism, genre criticism, social criticism, psychological criticism, structuralist criticism and feminism. There is an assumption throughout that you will be both a writer and a reader of criticism. One of the aims is also not to get bogged down in literary theory but to provide practical opportunities for reading in a variety of ways. The final chapter provides further practice at using critics, building on the previous chapters, as well as giving advice on exam preparation.

Reading and interpreting poetry

It's important to know right from the start what you are trying to do when you read poetry. It's no good just launching into poems assuming that you'll make sense of each one as it comes along. This book will support a view of reading and interpretation known as 'engaged reflection'. This approach will enable you to develop good habits of reading and interpretation as well as meet the assessment objectives laid down for AS and A level.

'Engaged reflection' involves two connected aspects of reading:

1 The engagement: like all good engagements there is a commitment to what you are doing. 'Engaging with the poem' means that you 'get into it', you enjoy it, you let it trigger off emotions and thoughts, you respond to what it is saying, you care about it. Rather like when you are watching a good film, you are simply carried away by the action – although you may wish to challenge this comparison.
2 The reflection: reflections come back at you so that you see things in a way that you didn't before. Really this is just a metaphor to explain that you become aware of what you are experiencing or are engaged in so that you are able to make comments on what is causing the experience. Again, if this was about films then reflection means remaining aware enough so that you are not mindlessly absorbed by the action.

How to get engaged

Connect the poem with things that you know about people and about the world. If, for example, you are reading a love poem you might think about declaration of love and, perhaps, your experience of it at first hand or otherwise. For example, when people say the words 'I love you' in soaps or discuss it on problem pages. Initially, let the poem trigger these thoughts so that you can 'connect' with the poem. Then:

■ Ask the poem questions and give your own answers
■ Get into the characters' motivations

- Record how you think the poem makes you feel even if you don't know why
- Give way to the associations that arise in you
- Don't feel the pressure to be intellectual too soon.

How to reflect

The question to ask is: 'What is making you think these things?' This means looking in the text for specific devices – the familiar techniques such as metaphor, imagery, rhyme, antithesis, etc. But it also means looking at the context of the poem and your reading. That is, you will need to look outside the poem and examine the ideas and attitudes that you find there. So, you might know something of the poet's life and the circumstances in which he/she wrote the poem or it might be that the poem has called forth from you some stereotype. In which case you need to reflect further on the nature of the stereotype and your relationship with it. Reflection is like holding a mirror up to yourself as you read the poem.

ACTIVITY 2

In the following example, a reader has responded to Tennyson's *Break, Break, Break*. The reader knows that the poem is Tennyson's reaction to the death of his friend, Arthur Hallam, in 1833. The response is broken down into the two phases of engagement and reflection. Continue each part in your own way (or you may wish to start again) but, whatever you do, make sure that you reflect upon and expand upon your initial responses.

Engagement

1 *Rhythm of waves*

Break, Break, Break

2 *As in a 'broken heart'?*

Break, break, break,
　　On thy cold gray stones, O Sea!
And I would that my tongue could utter
　　The thoughts that arise in me.

3 *I can hear some ancient BBC voice saying 'Break, break, break', slowly and coldly.*

4 *Cold, bleak, blank – emotionally and literally.*

O well for the fisherman's boy,
　　That he shouts with his sister at play!
O well for the sailor lad,
　　That he sings in his boat on the bay!

6 *He sounds bitter here – 'it's alright for them!'*

5 *The exclamation marks surprise me.*

And the stately ships go on
　　To their haven under the hill;
But O for the touch of a vanished hand,
　　And the sound of a voice that is still!

8 *Could men express that then? Was Tennyson gay?*

7 *'Stately' – does that mean 'big' or 'important'?*

Break, break, break,
　　At the foot of thy crags, O sea!
But the tender grace of a day that is dead
　　Will never come back to me.

10 *Tennyson wouldn't have spoken like that.*

9 *Repeats it again.*

11 *Self-pity?*

Reflection

1 and **2** It's good to consider that a line has more than one meaning. Maybe the poet wishes that he could 'break'? He certainly sees himself as fragile, in contrast to the sea which, along with its 'cold, gray stones' presents a united front. Is Tennyson conscious of playing his role as 'broken hearted'? Note that the monosyllables of 'break, break, break' would tend to slow it down, in keeping with the mood of the poem.

3 This is purely associational for the reader but it helps the reader to hear the poem. On further reflection, the only words in the first stanza that have more than one syllable are 'utter' and 'arise', and this is what the poem is surely about – the <u>expression</u> of his grief.

4 Are the sea and the stones more of an outward expression of his grief than what he can actually say? Or are they indifferent in their relentless continuation? Why not both?

If you wish to follow up this activity immediately, turn to page 85.

Going public – how to make use of your associations

You may have had your doubts about the engagement part of the above procedure. Perhaps you can see little use for any kind of personal response because what ultimately gets you marks are those clever bits that have mostly been fed to you by your teacher. In a sense this somewhat cynical view is true but you will never get beyond this dependence if you don't risk a more personal approach. This is because examiners are interested in your views as an independent reader, not as a swallower/consumer and regurgitator of fixed ideas.

Many of your early responses to a poem will probably not find their way into your final response, especially if the final response takes the form of a formal essay. Don't be afraid to discard your earlier thoughts – you should expect your thoughts about a poem to grow and change all the time. But instead of just rejecting those early ideas it's best if you can reflect on what it was that led to them.

If one of your early responses is a personal association of some kind, then it is unlikely that an examiner or anyone else will give you any credit for repeating it. What you have to do is make that response publicly negotiable. That is, you need to convert it into a statement that others can argue with. So, for example, if the poem triggers off the memory of an elderly relative of yours, you need to work out what it is between yourself and the poem that is triggering off this memory. Once you have converted the association into a form that others can argue with you are in a position to justify your argument or be beaten down by others. Here are some examples:

Association	Publicly negotiable explanation
Memory of elderly relative	poem stereotypes old people poem is sentimental poem tries to elicit same feelings as you felt about the relative

Some books will steer you away from the engagement part of responding and will see it as unnecessary. But with practice you will find that engagement opens up responses you never knew you had in you and frees you from the pressure to intellectualise too soon. After all, poetry is about feeling as well as thinking.

ACTIVITY 3

Try responding to any of the poems in this book in the way suggested above. You might start with either of the two poems by D. H. Lawrence on page 46, *Digging* by Seamus Heaney (page 60) or *A Slumber Did my Spirit Seal* by William Wordsworth (page 58). Convert any associations into publicly negotiable statements, as in the above table.

Variety of readings

How are different interpretations possible?

This section introduces the main idea of this book – that poetry can be interpreted in many different ways. Seeing these different perspectives involves thinking creatively and opening up your mind to alternative points of view. This often involves the idea of context which has taken on major importance in A level specifications. Context used to mean the same as background but it now means much more. Context can include:

- How would a woman read this poem?
- How would it have been read at the time it was published?
- How does the poem compare with similar poems written before and after?
- What if the poem were being read in a different culture?

It's best to start off thinking that context doesn't provide answers – it opens up possibilities. The next few activities explore those possibilities.

Learning to drive 1: if a traffic light was a poem

ACTIVITY 4

Key Skills: Communication – discussion

How many different ways are there of looking at traffic lights? On your own and then in a group explore your ideas based on the following perspectives:

- The point of view of drivers – what feelings are aroused?
- What are traffic lights similar to? How, for example, do they compare with lights at a level crossing or other lights that tell you what to do?
- The significance of the colours – what do they symbolise in other contexts?
- The ideas of 'stopping' and 'going' – what connotations do these words have?
- The designers of traffic lights – why didn't they put the green and the orange on at the same time, for example?

COMMENTARY   Here is a selection of possible perspectives:

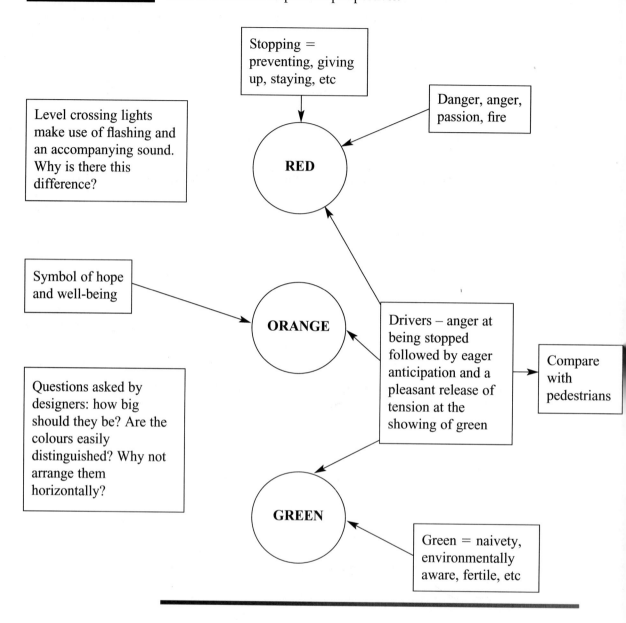

Stopping = preventing, giving up, staying, etc

Danger, anger, passion, fire

Level crossing lights make use of flashing and an accompanying sound. Why is there this difference?

RED

Symbol of hope and well-being

ORANGE

Drivers – anger at being stopped followed by eager anticipation and a pleasant release of tension at the showing of green

Compare with pedestrians

Questions asked by designers: how big should they be? Are the colours easily distinguished? Why not arrange them horizontally?

GREEN

Green = naivety, environmentally aware, fertile, etc

ACTIVITY 5

Imagine that a friend of yours has written a poem that goes simply: 'Red – orange – green'. How would you interpret it? What title would you give it? Use some of the above ideas or other ideas of your own.

ACTIVITY 6

In a pair unscramble the following words to create a short poem that will form the central focus of this book. The poem is called *Valentile*. Consider: punctuation, images, overall theme and form. Although there is no 'correct' answer you will find Jeremy Hughes' version of the poem on p11.

hands	We	baked	Two	glaze
in	fused	one	the	firing
clays	under	as	touch	

ACTIVITY 7

Key Skills: Communication – reading

This activity takes a different approach to the idea that poets and their poetry can be read in a variety of ways. Read the newspaper article below called 'Establishment Bard Tops List'. The article considers the suitability of several poets for the position of Poet Laureate – official poet to the Queen. How many ways of judging the poets does the article consider? For example, the opening paragraph judges Andrew Motion in terms of his acceptability to mainstream society. Count these ways of judging and think up suitable names for them.

THE INDEPENDENT ON SUNDAY
1 NOVEMBER 1998
by Marguerite Jones

ESTABLISHMENT BARD TOPS LIST

ANDREW MOTION is emerging as front-runner to succeed Ted Hughes as Poet Laureate, *writes Marguerite Jones.* The biographer of Keats, prolific poet and professor of creative writing at East Anglia is seen as an Establishment figure who would be highly acceptable for the job.

Some sense that Professor Motion's application for the post was submitted 16 months ago: he wrote a poem on the death of Diana, Princess of Wales, published in the *Times* on the day of her funeral.

Should he be appointed, it will disappoint those who believe the next Poet Laureate represents an opportunity for the position to reflect Britain today: multicultural, with women playing a far greater role in public life.

Wendy Cope has been cited as a candidate by the *Independent*, the *Times*, and Peter Forbes, editor of the *Poetry Review*. "She is genuinely popular, funny and topical. She works very well to commission," Mr Forbes said. "She is something of a female Betjeman; wry and very much a public poet."

Also a contender is Fleur Adcock, who achieved notoriety with her "In the dream I was kissing John Prescott" line of verse.

Benjamin Zephaniah, whose verse draws heavily on Afro-Caribbean speech and culture, and Derek Walcott, who hails from St Lucia, are also considered candidates who would bring a breath of fresh air to the job.

One of the most popular poets of the age, the Nobel Prize-winner Seamus Heaney, is ineligible because he is Irish. But as Mr Forbes puts it: "Might Number 10 think that Seamus Heaney as Poet Laureate would give a boost to the peace process?"

Candidates who would win the youth vote are Simon Armitage and performance-poet John Hegley.

COMMENTARY   The reference to Motion's poem about Diana suggests that poetry can be judged by its effect on the real world – how useful the poem is, in this case, for overcoming grief and later, with reference to Heaney, for helping the peace process in Northern Ireland. But the next paragraph suggests that poetry should represent society as it is today – 'multicultural' and influenced by women. The paragraph about Wendy Cope implies that public popularity would be a suitable criterion. The phrase 'a breath of fresh air' takes originality – poetry's ability to provide a fresh angle – to be important. Seamus Heaney's exclusion on the grounds of nationality raises the question of race and ethnicity as do the references to Afro-Caribbean poets. Finally, the passage considers 'the youth vote' – raising the question that different groups of readers may judge poetry in different ways.

The next activity will suggest how a number of different readings can grow from personal responses.

ACTIVITY 8

Imagine that a poem contains the line: 'The red ball fell from the child's torn hand.'

1 Respond to each word in as much detail as possible, creating associations with as many words as you can. You may wish to exclude function words such as 'the' and 'from'.

2 Combine or link as many of these ideas as you can.

3 From the various combinations, come up with two or three ways of reading this line.

COMMENTARY   One set of possible associations with this line is as follows:

(The)	red	blood (thus sacrifice, wound and life)	sunset, bloody world
	ball	*mandala*, world, sun, spinning	
(from the)	fell	failure, the Fall of Man, descent	the world created or discarded
	child's	innocence, ignorance, weakness, simplicity, Christ, Out of the mouths of babes, birth	
	torn	wounded (by malice or accident), Christ's hands, the wounded hero	
	hand	the making part of the body, the potter's hand	

mandala – Sanskrit for 'magic circle', an intricate symmetrical pattern used for meditation.

adapted from R. Skelton, *Poetic Truth*

The point here is that a response to poetry can grow from many possible combinations of these ideas. The line may equally be a lament for the world's lost innocence or the failure of Christ to save the world.

ACTIVITY 9

This activity provides the basis for much of what follows later in this book. Copy out the short poem below and write your responses using the method shown on pages 4–5 (engaged reflection), perhaps adapting it to any personal style of responding that you have developed in the course of your study of literature. Remember to read the poem aloud and experiment with different tones of voice: satisfied, gently humorous, frustrated or dreamy? Then tackle the activities that follow.

Valentile

We touch under glaze,
hands fused in the firing.
Two clays baked as one.

Here are five readings of Jeremy Hughes' poem *Valentile* from a range of perspectives represented in this book:

Reading 1
The poem refers to a period when the poet's relationship with his partner was just beginning and he felt that he had no chance of making it work. Thus, the relationship is secret and can only take place under a glaze – under the surface, not overtly, or possibly under an illusion of success for which 'glaze' is a metaphor. Similarly, it is only hands and nothing more significant (like bodies) that can ever be 'fused in the firing'; the poet fears that it will always remain at this level. 'Fused' may also have the sense of 'gone wrong', as in the expression 'blown a fuse'. Because the poet feels that the relationship is doomed from the start, he expresses his greatest wish, that they will be 'as one', in terms of this final cliché. The wish is as unreal as the romantic films with which it is associated. All of this is expressed through the metaphor of making a tile because the poet is interested in crafts such as ceramics and carpentry.

Reading 2
The poem is written in the tradition of comic love poetry as, for example, in Carol Ann Duffy's *Valentine* in which she enthuses about the possibilities of an onion as a valentine. The poem achieves this effect by means of its word play on 'valentine' which, because of the word 'tile', allows the poet to extend the love-as-ceramics metaphor. The allusion to the cliché 'two hearts beat as one' in the final line keeps the poem 'light' and therefore comic. The poem also takes the form of a haiku, a poem that traditionally created a 'word picture'; here a tile 'fixes' the relationship that the poem describes, rather like a picture fixes its images. So the form of the poem reinforces its theme.

Reading 3
The poem is about male power which confuses a love-interest with a personal interest in ceramics. It appears to be a light-hearted valentine but the poet is intent on cleverly displaying his ability to extend a metaphor ('fused') and use word-play ('valentile') all neatly wrapped up in a haiku. Any mention of the recipient of the poem (who is known to be female) has been cleverly eliminated by the use of the pronoun 'we' – notice how, with

typical male egotism, the poet assumes they are together (in the 'we') even before they are fused: and he presumes to speak for both of them throughout, using plurals until he reaches the sinister 'one'. This word pretends a romantic union but it can only refer to the 'one' who has been dominant throughout – the poet himself. The finality of his over-confident assertions is emphasised by the monosyllabic words of the last line.

Reading 4

This is a poem about sex and death. It is disguised as a love poem and the word-play on 'valentine' also distracts readers from these darker meanings. 'Tiles' are put on the surface of things but this poem secretly celebrates what goes on underneath, hence 'under glaze'. Interestingly, if you take the 'l' out of 'glaze' you get 'gaze', so again the 'l' plays a part in hiding the poet's true feelings; he secretly wants to expose his desire to the 'gaze' of others. The second line obviously refers to sexual intercourse, with 'fused' suggesting a physical joining and the intensity of passion. Again the true nature of this passion is concealed in the alliteration on the 'f' with 'fire': what the poet really wants to say is 'fuck' but the word is too direct for a valentine. The final line hides behind the suggested cliché 'two hearts beat as one' but again its purpose is much darker. 'Clay', by association with 'earth', suggests 'death'; such is the intensity of the passion that the poet sees it as final. In other words the poet can see nothing in life as intense as this 'fire', so it is like a death, total obliteration of the self.

Reading 5

In this poem romantic love, and the bonding that it entails, is a metaphor for the poet's views on manual work. Here physical work is praised as if the poet were in love with it, hence 'valentine' becomes 'valentile'. The work of the tiler is chosen because it involves creation from the most basic of ingredients and processes: 'clay' and 'firing'; and so it stands for the creation of artefacts from natural materials. The end result is the unifying effect that this act of creation has on the people involved. 'Hands' carry out the work, with 'fused' emphasising the unity they achieve by working together in the firing. The fact that there are two 'clays' at the end (and not 'tiles') suggests that not only does work unite people but it is also a constant reminder that all humans are mortal.

Reading 6

The poem seems to be built around the following opposition:

the idea of two:	*unity or oneness:*
('We', 'hands', 'two' 'clays')	('one', 'fused', 'firing')

The poem describes the process of becoming united through love – of moving from the two to the one. It develops through three stages: from initial contact ('touch' – 'glaze'), to the intensity of passion ('fused') to the final state of unity ('baked'). These three stages, marked by the three lines of the poem, show the move from one side of the opposition to the other. Each line in itself also moves from the idea of 'two' (at the beginning of each line) towards this state of unity (at the end of each line).

ACTIVITY 10

Key Skills: Communication – reading

Here are some brief descriptions of various ways of reading or interpreting poetry. Each one will be expanded in the chapters of this book. However, it should be emphasised that these are not the only ways of reading poetry. The poet's own views on *Valentile* are given on p83.

Match the readings of *Valentile* above with the descriptions of ways of reading below. Photocopy the readings and underline evidence that supports your view.

Genre Criticism

Genre refers to the form or type of writing that a poet has produced. In the case of poetry this includes: sonnet, lyric, ballad, haiku, etc. This kind of criticism describes an individual poet's use of the genre compared with its use by other poets in the past, emphasising similarities and differences in the form in connection with the poet's theme and context of writing.

Social Criticism

This kind of criticism sees the poem from the point of view of a particular social group; for example, the working class or a racial minority. Marxist criticism, in particular, was concerned with social class, and criticism from the point of view of racial minorities is sometimes called post-colonial criticism because it represents the views of countries that were formerly colonies of countries such as Britain, Spain and France.

Feminist Criticism

This method of reading considers poetry from the point of view of women. It might ask what the poem is actually saying about women and their relationship with men, whether or not the poem means to do this. It might also ask how a woman would read a poem differently from a man.

Structuralist Criticism

This approach suggests that literature is rather like language. It is built up from a network of contrasting concepts such as 'good' versus 'evil', 'life versus death'. These contrasts build to create the special meaning of the poem. Other structuralist approaches involve analyses of point of view, the organisation of time and putting sections of the poem into categories.

Psychological Criticism

This method looks at the underlying psychology behind the poem. This could involve the psychology of the poet, especially if built up over several poems. It could involve interpreting symbolism described by psychoanalysts such as Sigmund Freud or Carl Jung.

Biographical Criticism

Using this method a poem is interpreted in terms of events in the poet's life. For example, when interpretation of *The Rime of the Ancient Mariner* is seen to be connected with Coleridge's drug addiction, or when Milton's poetry is explained with reference to his blindness or the Civil War and Milton's belief in a republic.

The value of not knowing the answers

Studying poetry is probably unlike studying any other subject on the curriculum. Some subjects primarily require knowledge; that is you have to know something about something, as in the case of History and Geography. Some subjects require skills in which general principles are applied to new situations. But there are a few subjects that combine knowledge and skills with thinking and feeling, letting a part of yourself interact with the subject. Even more odd is that it is sometimes best not to try to understand every word of a poem. Perfect explanation would signal the end of poetry.

Good questions

One of the keys to reading poems is asking good questions. What is a good question? Good questions work in a similar way to good works of literature. You may have watched or listened to an expert being interviewed about a topical issue on the television or radio. When the expert says, 'That's a good question,' they usually mean that it's a difficult one to answer, that it makes them think hard about an important issue. It's the same with good poems: they don't give up their answers easily, even when you ask the right questions in the first place. Good answers, which are not necessarily the end of all discussion, arise from good questions. There is a strong case for saying that if you think you've got the complete answer to a poem, you probably haven't.

Throughout this book you will find questions in boxes like the one below for your consideration:

> **How do you ask good questions about poems?**

Summary

This chapter is central to the organisation of the whole book. It has suggested a method for reading poetry ('engaged reflection') and it has introduced the idea that it is always possible to interpret poetry in a variety of ways. The chapter ends with an exploration of the poem *Valentile* from five different perspectives.

Further Reading

Mike Fleming, 'Poetry and Drama: Not Waving but Drowning', in the *Secondary English Magazine*, Vol 2, No 4, April 1999. Considers dramatic approaches to interpretation. Aimed at GCSE teachers but a good place to start.

Angela Foulkes, Sue Rogers, Pat McNeill, *Key Skills in A Levels: English Literature*, The National Extension College, 2000.

Magnetic Poetry Kits. Available in many bookshops, these now come in many different sets for your fridge if you enjoy scrambled words before breakfast.

John Moss, 'Writing more than reading *To His Coy Mistress*', in the *Secondary English Magazine*, Vol 3, No 5, June 2000. Looks at various ways of reading this poem, but a demanding read in itself (for teachers).

2 The Full Story? Biographical Reading

The passion of your life becomes more vivid as a result of poetry

Valentile

We touch under glaze,
hands fused in the firing.
Two clays baked as one.

Biographical reading in action

Refers to a part of the poet's life

The poem refers to a period when the poet's relationship with his partner was just beginning and he felt that he had no chance of making it work. Thus, the relationship is secret and can only take place under a glaze – under the surface, not overtly, or possibly under an illusion of success for which 'glaze' is a metaphor. Even the title expresses the desire to hide the relationship. Similarly, it is only hands and nothing more significant (like bodies) that can ever be 'fused in the firing'; the poet fears that it will always remain at this level. 'Fused' may also have the sense of 'gone wrong', as in the expression 'blown a fuse'. Because the poet feels that the relationship is doomed from the start, he expresses his greatest wish, that they will be 'as one', in terms of this final cliché. The wish is as unreal as the romantic films with which it is associated. All of this is expressed through the metaphor of making a tile because the poet is interested in crafts such as ceramics and carpentry.

Connects biography with part of the poem

Note that the emphasis is primarily on the poem

Biography explains a specific word

Refers to use of language

The writer speculates about the poet's choice of words and biographical details

It is true to say that all creative writers put a little bit of their own lives into their writing. Often they put in a great deal. Incidents from the life of the author of a literary work are one of the most popular and memorable contexts of reading. It is often this biographical reading that sticks in the public imagination. For example, because some of Shakespeare's sonnets were addressed to a man there has been endless speculation about Shakespeare's sexual orientation. Similarly, people wanted to know what really happened between Sylvia Plath and Ted Hughes in the 1950s and 1960s and, when *Birthday Letters* was published in the late 1990s, this insight into Hughes' 'real' feelings was welcomed. But – there is good news and bad news as far as this method of reading is concerned. It is one of the most attractive methods yet also one of the most plagued with pitfalls.

One of the more serious pitfalls is to assume that biographies are factual and therefore fixed forever. The following article appeared in the *Guardian* in 1993:

A Poetic Injustice

Hysteria over the publication of Philip Larkin's *Letters and Life* culminated in calls for his poetry to be banned. Instead, a more subtle censorship has been undertaken: the quiet destruction of Larkin's literary reputation. MARTIN AMIS demands an end to the witch-hunt.

... In the early eighties, the common mind imagined Larkin as a reclusive yet twinkly drudge – bald, bespectacled, bicycle-clipped, slumped in a shabby library gaslit against the dusk. In the early nineties, we see a fuddled Scrooge and bigot, his singlet-clad form barely visible through a mephitis of alcohol, anality and spank magazines. The reaction against Larkin has been unprecedentedly violent, as well as unprecedentedly hypocritical, tendentious and smug. Its energy does not – could not – derive from literature ...

Guardian Weekend, 21 August, 1993

ACTIVITY 11

Key Skills: Communication – discussion

In a small group brainstorm reasons why, over time, views of a poet's life and work might change for the better or for the worse.

Biographical reading is attractive because:

- Real life events often feel like explanations. It's as if the poem has to connect with real life before it can make sense.
- Many readers feel secure if they can connect the poem with the poet.
- Biography can sometimes uncover the actual process of writing.

But biographical reading can be a trap because:

- It's too easy to assume that the 'I' in the poem or the persona created is the real life poet. It may just be the part they are playing on that particular day.
- Real life events often feel like explanations. But why should they be the end of the line of interpretation? Rather, they should send you back into the poem.
- This approach can imply that the biography is in some way more important than the poem because all the poem does is illustrate some aspect of the poet's life.

Poets and personas

It is important to be able to distinguish between poems directly about a poet's life experiences and poems in which a poet is not writing directly about himself; that is, where a persona is created. The table below gives examples of each kind:

About the 'real' poet	Feature an adopted persona
T. S. Eliot's *Ash Wednesday*	Shelley's *Ozymandias*
Thomas Hardy's poems of 1912–13	Coleridge's *The Rime of the Ancient Mariner*
Seamus Heaney's *Death of a Naturalist*	Grace Nichols' *The Fat Black Woman's Poems*
Tennyson's *Break Break Break*	Tennyson's *Ulysses*
Wordsworth's *The Prelude*	T. S. Eliot's *The Love Song of J. Alfred Prufrock*

There is more of an obligation to read poems of the left-hand column from a biographical perspective. But you should realise that the poet is still only creating an image of himself that may be confirmed or denied by other sources. Biographies, autobiographies, contemporary newspaper articles and interviews, for example, may create different images of the poet compared with the poem, and often make for interesting comparisons.

The addition of a biographical element into poems of the right-hand column can raise interesting possibilities – possibilities that send you into biographical speculation, hunting down information that might support your theory. For example, many readers have found elements of Coleridge himself in the figure of the Ancient Mariner and of Tennyson in Ulysses. And you don't have to be a professional critic to discover this for yourself.

ACTIVITY 12

Key Skills: Communication – reading; IT – different sources

The table below begins to make links between *The Rime of the Ancient Mariner* and aspects of Coleridge's life. Complete the table by doing some biographical research on Coleridge and don't be put off by the fact that many of the important events happened after Coleridge wrote the poem. Some sources of information are: the internet, encyclopaedias, introductions to anthologies, biographies and literary histories. For this activity you don't necessarily need to be studying the poem but it helps if you are. In brief, the poem tells the story of a sailor who embarks on a long sea journey. He then kills an albatross and undergoes a long and strange punishment at sea. Finally returning to land he repents his crime but is forced to tell his story forever.

Aspect of the poem	Aspect of Coleridge's life
Shooting an albatross	Taking opium
A nightmarish journey	
A man who goes around telling his story	
Solitude at sea	
Life in death	

Here are some of the biographical elements that emerge in other poets' work:

- *Shakespeare*: he wrote poems for his patron, the Earl of Southampton, and for the 'dark lady'.
- *John Milton*: Experience of revolution in England, position as a republican after the monarchy had been restored to the throne of England.
- *William Blake*: living through the Industrial Revolution, experience of visions as a child.
- *Samuel Coleridge*: feelings of guilt and other emotions arising from his opium addiction.
- *Alfred Lord Tennyson*: death of friend Arthur Hallam.
- *Elizabeth Barrett Browning*: falling in love with Robert Browning.
- *Wilfred Owen*: World War 1.
- *T. S. Eliot*: conversion to Catholicism.
- *Sylvia Plath*: relationship with mother and father, experience of a mental institution and 'treatment' for mental illness.
- *Philip Larkin*: lack of success with women – 'Deprivation is for me what daffodils were for Wordsworth'.
- *Seamus Heaney*: the experience of being from Northern Ireland.
- *Ted Hughes*: relationship with Sylvia Plath, Plath's suicide.
- *R. S. Thomas*: a Welsh nationalist living in remote rural communities.
- *Grace Nichols*: Caribbean childhood, moving to England, etc.
- *Carol Ann Duffy*: experiences of school, moving from Scotland to England.

ACTIVITY 13

Key Skills: Communication/IT – could be developed in many ways

Write a magazine article aimed at A level students about the ways in which poets put a part of themselves into their poetry. Here are some hints: you might like to refer to poets from the list above but you are also free to use encyclopaedias and other sources of information; what is your 'angle' going to be?

You might want, for example, to warn budding poets about what they might be about to reveal about themselves, or, you might express some of the dangers of biographical reading expressed in this chapter. Alternatively, you might want to argue that poetry is really a kind of therapy for people (i.e. the writers) with problems. Refer to lots of examples and keep it lively and humorous but with a serious edge.

Working backwards

The biggest danger with biographical reading is that you take elements of the poet's life to be neat answers to problems presented in the poems. The danger is compounded by the fact that biographical information is so readily available: it is likely to be the first information you come across when you research an author. It's as if you say, 'Oh, so that's why he wrote it … because he … did such and such or went to so and so'.

Tennyson's *Break, Break, Break* (page 5) is a case in point. If you read the poem without knowing about Tennyson's relationship with Arthur Hallam, you can pick up the essence of the sentiment behind the poem. If you know about Hallam, everything seems to slot into place – so much so that it can give you a false sense of having done with the poem. But biographical information cannot be considered an answer to the problems you discover in the poem. Information about a poet's life needs to be interpreted as much as the poems themselves because it is itself a construction for a particular purpose, context and audience. In Tennyson's case it makes sense to interpret the biographical information using the poem. In other words we can work out what kind of relationship the two men had by using the poem.

To avoid taking biographical information at face value it is sometimes worth looking at the biography before you look at the poetry so that you take a more critical view of the relationship between the two. It is also obviously important to be able to distinguish between fact and interpretation.

ACTIVITY 14

Key Skills: Communication – reading/discussion

Photocopy the following biographical fragments and highlight in one colour the parts that are about the poet. Choose another colour for parts that are about the poetry. Is the text all fact or is there some interpretation? Discuss how this might influence the way that you interpret the poetry.

Tony Harrison (1937–) was born in Leeds, the only son of a bakery worker, and attended Cross Flats County Primary, the local school.

Aged eleven, however, he won one of only a few scholarships to Leeds Grammar School, and thus began the transition from his original background to the world of intellectual aspiration, a tension which has remained his principal subject.

A. E. Housman (1859–1936) was the eldest son of seven children . . . of a prosperous solicitor practising in Bromsgrove, Worcestershire. The idealised rural Shropshire of Housman's poetry was thus the 'western horizon' of his childhood, eternally near and just out of reach.

from *The Reader's Companion to Twentieth Century Writers*, ed. P. Parker, Helicon, 1995

COMMENTARY The first of these extracts deals with facts until the very end when the word 'tension' signals the shift to interpretation of the poetry. You should be aware, however, that the 'facts' have been carefully chosen (from among the many other things that Harrison did as a child) to support the interpretation. The second extract moves from fact in the first sentence to interpretation in the second, especially in the words 'idealised' and 'eternally near and just out of reach' which is a metaphor suggesting Housman's emotional stance towards his subject. This shift is again almost imperceptible so that you tend to take for granted that what the text is saying is simply true. The effect of both biographies is to close down possibilities for interpretation rather than open them up.

ACTIVITY 15

Key Skills: IT – different sources/information

Referring to any poet you are studying, find out, using an encyclopedia or CD ROM, which life events the poet is most commonly associated with. Compare the entries of at least three sources. How much agreement is there between the sources? How might this influence the way that you read that poet's work?

> Does the biography interpret the poem or the poem interpret the biography?

ACTIVITY 16

Key Skills: Communication – reading

Biographies need to be interpreted. Read the following fragment about the life of a poet.

a Predict what kind of poetry the poet might have written. Justify your views. Where do your views come from?
b Research some of the poetry he has written and test your predictions.

James Kirkup

The son of a carpenter, Kirkup grew up at odds with his working-class environment in South Shields, County Durham. He wanted to be a dancer and then a poet, and was a solitary figure at South Shields Secondary School. He went on to Durham University then, refusing military service, spent the Second World War as a lumberjack and farm labourer.

COMMENTARY The diagram below shows the kind of thinking that might lie behind interpretation of the first mini-biography above.

James Kirkup (1918–)

| | Might have views about the value of working-class craftsmanship | Hang-ups about expectations of working class? |

| Gender issues could be important because this is against stereotype, especially in that community |

The son of a *carpenter, Kirkup grew up at odds with his working-class environment* in South Shields, County Durham. He wanted to be *a dancer and then a poet,* and was *a solitary figure at South Shields Secondary School.* He went on to *Durham University,* then, *refusing military service,* spent the Second World War as *a lumberjack and farm labourer.*

| Strong contrast between intellectual and manual |

| Idealism may be expressed in his poetry |

| May feel that he is misunderstood |

The above analysis shows that the biography is not a simple statement of fact but a selection or construction that helps to create an image of the poet.

ACTIVITY 17

Now do the same with the following biographical fragments.

Elizabeth Barrett Browning (1806–61) was born of wealthy parents a few miles from Durham. From the age of 15 she suffered from a tubercular complaint although there is also speculation that she was crippled by a fall when riding. Towards the end of her life she used pain-killing drugs and became dependent on them. She met and married Robert Browning against her father's wishes and ran away to live with him in Florence. She gave birth to a son at the age of 43.

Alexander Pope (1688–1744) was born into a wealthy Catholic family. He suffered ill health from boyhood which left him a cripple for most of his life. His education was as a result not as complete as it might have been and this left him vulnerable to attacks from his critics, especially regarding his edition of the works of Shakespeare. He was known as an ill-tempered man whose work tends to be admired rather than greatly loved.

Do your speculations about these biographies lead you towards any other kinds of readings in this book?

ACTIVITY 18

Key Skills: IT – present information

You might follow up the above activity by
either

a Reading some of the work by these poets to
test your hypotheses,
b Checking some of your 'readings' by
referring to more lengthy accounts of these
poets' lives, or

c Creating your own mini-biography for a poet
that you are studying.

Can you write so that it suggests some of the
qualities that are apparent in the poetry? It
would be interesting to attempt a biography
after six poems and then after twelve, and so on.
Or try writing biographies aimed at two
different types of readers – children and
feminists, for example.

Finding the 'real' poet?

ACTIVITY 19

In the poem below, what can you read of
Hardy's relationship with his wife who had
recently died? Consider:

a The poem's mood
b 'Where' the action of the poem takes place

c Hardy's relationship with his wife when she
was alive
d What Hardy now feels.

After a Journey

Hereto I come to view a voiceless ghost;
Whither, O whither will its whim now draw me?
Up the cliff, down, till I'm lonely, lost,
And the unseen waters' ejaculations awe me.
Where you will next be there's no knowing,
Facing round about me everywhere,
With your nut-coloured hair,
And gray eyes, and rose-flush coming and going.

Yes: I have re-entered your olden haunts at last;
Through the years, through the dead scenes I have tracked you;
What have you now found to say of our past –
Scanned across the dark space wherein I have lacked you?
Summer gave us sweets, but autumn wrought division?
Things were not lastly as firstly well
With us twain, you tell?
But all's closed now, despite Time's derision.

I see what you are doing: you are leading me on
To the spots we knew when we haunted here together,
The waterfall, above which the mist-bow shone
At the then fair hour in the then fair weather,
And the cave just under, with a voice still so hollow
That it seems to call out to me from forty years ago,
When you were all aglow,
And not the thin ghost that I now frailly follow!

Ignorant of what there is flitting here to see,
The waked birds preen and the seals flop lazily;
Soon you will have, Dear, to vanish from me,
For the stars close their shutters and the dawn whitens hazily.
Trust me, I mind not, though Life lours,
The bringing me here; nay, bring me here again!
I am just the same as when
Our days were a joy, and our paths through flowers.

Thomas Hardy

ACTIVITY 20

Key Skills: Communication – presentation

1. Now return to the poem in the light of this comment from *The Cambridge Guide to English Literature*: 'Emma Hardy died in 1912, and the poems that followed, in *Satires of Circumstance* (1914), reflect his feeling of both loss and guilt – he deeply regretted the strained relations of the last years.'

2 Using the model provided by the analysis of *Valentile* at the beginning of this chapter, write your own analysis of *After a Journey*.

Remember to balance your analysis with reflections about Hardy's relationship with his wife, and the language of the poem.

3 Compare your reading of this poem with the one given below. Photocopy (and enlarge) both the poem and this reading. Create a display by cutting up the reading into sentences or other units and mapping them on to the appropriate places in the poem using arrows. Is it possible to do the same thing with your own reading?

The poem brings one in on the crest of a wave of recovery; yet it does so with a tenderness, an intimacy, and a vulnerability that are set in a flint-like realism. Hardy, on his lover's journey, finds that the voice that leads him now is not the woman's travelling on the breeze (as in *The Voice*), but the soliloquies of the waters and the hollow plash of the cascade in the darkness – the darkness which is both in the real scene and in the landscape of his mind. Though the ghost is voiceless, it is the clearest he has felt her yet: astonishingly vivid, and as if in the flesh, mistress in her own place. He has to attend her in that place and unflinchingly face the questions that must be asked – but are barely answered. As so often, Hardy expresses in his broken lines and awkward inversions the inner distress of his heart. He knows that the questions are unanswerable; indeed, he evades the answers by putting them as questions in the voiceless Emma's mouth, with remote archaisms like 'wrought' and 'twain' to distance them. All is closed and he cannot go back. Time laughs wryly; but it does not necessarily laugh last.

For just as Hardy originally wrote 'soothed' instead of 'closed', one senses a healing beginning in the third stanza. 'I see what you are doing': he begins to understand. The experience is set in the cradle of time: 'Hereto I come . . .' 'Through the years, through the dead scenes . . .' 'it seems to call out to me from forty years ago . . .', and he can see her, in one sentence, as the girl who was 'all aglow', but who is now, like him, becoming 'thin' and 'frail'. From his vantage point he can see the reality and quality of their love as it was (or as he feels it was) which not even the tragic later years can destroy. It was the core of his life, the central and sovereign moment which has ruled it ever since. So as the horizon lightens, his darkness and his burden lighten . . .

By the end of this poem he is almost sprightly, fully in command; and he makes the tremendous claim that he is:

> ... just the same as when
> Our days were a joy, and our paths through flowers.

Can this really be so? And were the young couple really aware, in that summer forty years gone, of the 'rareness, ripeness, richness,' of those moments, as he sees them now looking back?

Joanna Cullen Brown, A Journey into Thomas Hardy's Poetry

You will find further examples of this kind of reading on page 61 and page 91.

Behind the mask

A common mistake is to assume that biographical information is somehow superior to the poetry. Poetry may seem to speak less directly and be altogether more difficult to understand. Biography, by contrast, is often an easy kind of interpretation to grasp and – importantly – you usually come across it after you have read the poetry, so that it feels like explanation. But it is also important to use the poem to read the biography.

In the above activity featuring the Hardy poem, the relationship between the poem and the biography was rather literal. In the poem Hardy was describing feelings and experiences he had actually had. Getting behind the poet's mask is, however, not always as straight forward as this.

ACTIVITY 21

Key Skills: Communication – discussion

Read and respond to the following poem by Carol Ann Duffy. In a small group predict what kind of biographical information might help to explain the ideas in the poem. Here are some suggestions:

- The poet's interest in astronomy
- The poet finding her grandmother dead in bed
- Coming from Scotland and living in England
- Having two pet cats
- Having had a university education
- Working as a landlord for ten years.

Room

One chair to sit in,
A greasy dusk wrong side of the tracks,
And watch the lodgers' lights come on in the other rooms.

No curtains yet. A cool light bulb
Waiting for a moth. Hard silence.
The roofs of terraced houses stretch from here to how many months.

Room. One second-hand bed
To remind of a death, somewhen. Room.
Then clouds the colour of smokers' lungs. Then what.

In a cold black window, a face
Takes off its glasses and stares out again.
Night now; the giftless moon and a cat pissing on a wall. £90pw.

Carol Ann Duffy

The following extract is taken from Sean O'Brien's *The Deregulated Muse*. It contains biographical information about the poet Carol Ann Duffy that can be used to interpret her poetry. In other words the extract sets up ideas that can be tested by reading the poems. In this sense it is a kind of script for reading the poem.

ACTIVITY 22

1 Photocopy O'Brien's commentary on Duffy and colour code it for fact and interpretation. Does O'Brien attempt to blur the difference between the two? Then respond to O'Brien in the same way as the mini-biographies on page 19.

2 Use this information to re-read *Room*. Then photocopy and annotate the poem in the light of O'Brien's comments.

Like several of the most striking poets now at work in England, Carol Ann Duffy has Celtic ancestry and a Catholic background ... The great emigrant cities of Glasgow (her birthplace) and Liverpool (where she studied) stand behind her work, and she has written of her childhood as 'an emigration' – part of that series of interior economic *diasporae* which led the Scots south (to Stafford in the case of Duffy's family) in search of work. Such displacements, as many would testify, make for a complicated unease in those fallen among the English ... Neither uprooted or rootless, but not having taken root, Duffy can stand as an emigrant in the country of which she is technically a citizen. This state of affairs may matter less to the increasingly mobile and often indifferently *deracinated* English, on the move in much (though not all) of England, than to the immigrant from the militarily (if not imaginatively) conquered periphery. The edge of estrangement is usually somewhere to hand in Duffy's work: it is part of what enables her to dramatise the experience of a wide variety of other strangers, many of them born here, who find themselves abroad in contemporary England.

diasporae – the spreading out of a race through emigration;
deracinated – had its roots taken away.

COMMENTARY

Duffy's poem may have triggered speculation about rented rooms as a student in some poor area of a large city. But there are also suggestions of loneliness, isolation and depression. However, it is best not to think too literally – after all, there is nothing to suggest that this was Duffy's personal experience. Perhaps one of the points of the poem is that it could be anyone's experience. O'Brien makes use of the fact that Duffy's family moved from Scotland to Staffordshire, connecting this with ideas such as 'estrangement' and 'strangers'. This part of his commentary is opinion and it bridges the gap between the poetry and the biographical facts.

From poem to biography and back

The relationship between poems and biographies is a two-way thing:

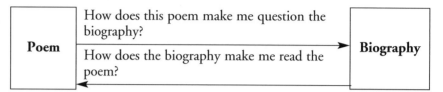

ACTIVITY 23

Use the following autobiographical fragment about Duffy to form your own reading of some of Duffy's poems that you may be studying. If you are not studying Duffy, try reading *Room* using the fragment, discussing any issues that arise with a partner. Can you, in other words, create an interpretative bridge between these biographical facts and the poetry? You may need to do some research into *Alice in Wonderland*.

> I cannot recall either of my parents reading for pleasure. The house I grew up in – rented from my father's employers – was virtually bookless. A Pear's *Cyclopaedia,* a mother-of-pearl prayer book, a *Brief History of Glasgow*, are all that I can squeeze from my memory; until I began to read myself. And once I started to read, I stayed reading. Before me now I have my first 'real' book, Lewis Carroll's *Alice's Adventures in Wonderland*, inscribed to me by my paternal grandfather in August, 1962. As one who has regularly lost other presents – rings, watches, and so on – it is significant to me that I still possess it. I loved *Alice*. It is the first book that I remember reading all the way through alone – as heady an experience as one's first cigarette – and it changed me. Here was a world to live in, simply through words. Given my strict and undoubtedly clichéd working-class, Catholic background, here was *escape*. Mad Hatters and pools of tears. Language.
>
> Ed. Antonia Fraser, *The Pleasure of Reading*

Summary

This chapter has emphasised that biographical reading needs to be undertaken with caution. Biographies contain opinion as well as fact and they are already interpretations of poetry. They should be read actively in conjunction with poetry and not simply as answers to the 'problem' of poetry. Often they are a link into the broader and complex issue of the historical context of the poem.

Further Reading

Peter Parker, *The Reader's Companion to Twentieth Century Writers*, Fourth Estate Ltd, 1995. A useful starting point.

Biographical fragments, as well as longer works, abound in libraries and all kinds of study guides. Always bear in mind when they were written, by whom, and for what purpose.

3 Changing Traditions

… it remains true that a writer's attitude towards form, which is inescapably the first thing we notice when we approach his work, is a reliable guide to his attitudes in general.

John Wain, *Professing Poetry*, 1977

Valentile

We touch under glaze,
hands fused in the firing.
Two clays baked as one.

Genre criticism in action

States the tradition the poem is working in →

Explains what makes the poem 'comic' →

← Makes a comparison with a similar kind of text

Refers to use of language →

Explains the form of the poem and its connection with the theme →

The poem is written in the tradition of comic love poetry as, for example, in Carol Ann Duffy's *Valentine* in which she enthuses about the possibilities of an onion as a valentine. The poem achieves this effect by means of its word play on 'valentine' which, because of the word 'tile', allows the poet to extend the love-as-ceramics metaphor. The allusion to the cliché 'two hearts beat as one' in the final line keeps the poem 'light' and therefore comic. The poem also takes the form of a haiku, a poem that traditionally created a 'word picture'; here a tile 'fixes' the relationship that the poem describes, rather like a picture fixes its images. So the form of the poem reinforces its theme.

When someone says 'poetry' what do you expect it to sound like? What do you expect it to look like? It's questions like these that will lead you into considering form and genre – the shape of the container into which the 'meanings' of the poetry are poured (a useful but not entirely accurate metaphor). This chapter focuses on that container, the shapes it has taken, and how you and the poet can make those shapes influence the way that you read.

One of the problems with poetry is perhaps that we have become less used to what to expect of certain forms of poetry compared with, say, films or computer games. Feature films are usually between an hour and a half and two hours long; if it's a horror movie you expect certain ingredients, and there are many other genres most adult viewers are familiar with. When you become really familiar with a genre, it's amazing how sensitive you can become to subtle changes in form, especially, for example, when the rules start to be broken.

Perhaps the most popular expectations of poetry are that it rhymes and it uses unusual or old-fashioned language compared with the language of daily life. But these observations will not take us very far, and – besides – they are often proved wrong!

ACTIVITY 24

Key Skills: Communication – discussion

In a pair think of a film or computer game genre. Brainstorm as many features of that genre as you can. Can you think of examples where the conventions of the genre have been altered in some way? What is the effect of doing this? How does it affect your perception of the film/computer game?

'Tradition' is not a word that usually inspires personal response or original thinking. The word carries a lot of baggage with it, baggage that you need to unpack and study in detail before you can make any progress at all, so it would seem. But all tradition means is that poets don't write in a vacuum; they are influenced, whether they like it or not, by the poetry that has gone before them, and sometimes they are consciously reacting against it. Some critics believe that the poets of every age are reacting against the poetry of the previous age so that tradition is constantly changing and reforming itself to suit the spirit of the age. All you really need to ask of a poem is 'What kind of thing is this?' and 'What similar things have been written?'

If you still think that genre or form just lead you into laborious tasks such as working out rhyme patterns, structures and rhythms, then consider this. Recognition of genre sets up *expectations* in the reader, expectations that can be met or deliberately thwarted by the text. Just as when you go to see a film, your ideas about the ending of the film will be influenced by the kind of film you consider it to be. Do you, for example, expect the hero to get the girl? Do you expect the villains to be defeated but also to be left with an element of doubt so that the way for a sequel is left open? Often, a good piece of art will satisfy some of your expectations but leave others unfulfilled. What you discover about genre can help you to interpret a text but it will often not provide neat answers. Clearly, questions about genre open up further questions as well as close some of them down.

One of the key words in this chapter is expectation. This is because genre communicates something about the context in which the poem was produced to create a series of expectations in the reader. Much of the business of appreciating poetry is about learning what to expect. These expectations will form the core of this chapter.

ACTIVITY 25

Key Skills: Communication – discussion

In a small group discuss what the forms below mean to you, without looking them up:

Sonnet   Epic   Lyric/free verse   Ballad/narrative poetry

Parody   Haiku

1 Think of examples of each kind that you may have already read.
2 Explain what you think are the essential ingredients of each one.
3 Rank order them from 'old' to 'new' in terms of when they were popular.
4 At this stage you may have to do some research into the 'correct' definitions of the forms. What expectations do you have of the way that you might respond to each one? For example, do you expect to:

- Jog along with the rhythm?
- Get drawn into an argument?
- Be reminded of other stories you have heard?
- See an old idea from a new angle?
- Admire the poet's concise use of language?
- Get some insight into the poet's life/character/relationships?
- Laugh?
- Experience a special moment with the poet or his persona? (see page 17)
- Follow an ancient story?
- Appreciate a brief picture in words?

COMMENTARY

Sonnet: This is a fourteen line poem, traditionally about love and first written in thirteenth century Italy. It became fashionable in England in the sixteenth century. Its language is densely woven and frequently draws on the development of an argument. It is covered in detail in the next section.

Epic: This is a narrative poem usually of considerable length, recounting great events and written in a formally grand style. It is often in rhyming couplets. For example, Milton's *Paradise Lost* and, in recent years Derek Walcott's *Omeros*.

Lyric/free verse: Lyrical poetry is usually much less grand in style and much shorter than the above. It often recounts a significant moment or feeling. Free verse often appears to be free form and is particularly associated with the experimentation of the twentieth century. Philip Larkin, W. H. Auden and Wilfred Owen often wrote in this way. Be careful not to get free verse confused with blank verse; the latter is often used in epics and refers to poetry that does not rhyme as, for example, in *Paradise Lost*.

Ballad/narrative poetry: Ballads are often part of the oral tradition so that authorship is frequently unknown. They are written as songs, are often set to music and have regular patterns of rhyme and rhythm that pull you along with the story using sparse but significant imagery; for example, *Sir Patrick Spens* (anonymous).

Parody: This can take any form it likes but will essentially imitate another form in order to amuse.

Haiku: Derived from the Japanese, this three line picture-poem has been written in English since the sixteenth/seventeenth centuries although it is often thought to be a modern form. There is more on this on page 83.

ACTIVITY 26

Key Skills: Communication – reading

Apply the above categories to the poems in this book. Which one does not appear?

ACTIVITY 27

Key Skills: Communication – reading

In a small group think of a poem that you all know or that you are studying. Discuss the consequences of changing the poem from its current form to another one.

A brief encounter with sonnets

To use genre-based criticism it helps if the writer is using a well-established tradition such as the sonnet form. This allows you to look for variation in the traditional form and connect this with the new context, subject or purpose. But you should never assume that so called free verse is completely free – there is always some reference to what has gone before even if it's just the poet rejecting what has gone before!

Sonnets have been written notably by: Spenser, Shakespeare, Milton, Wordsworth, Keats, Elizabeth Barrett Browning, W. B. Yeats, Douglas Dunn . . . to name but a few. This obviously means that when you study a sonnet, it's worth considering where it stands in relation to others that have been written.

Then come the important questions:

■ Is the poet conforming to the tradition of a particular kind of sonnet or is it being developed or changed in some way?
■ If the poet is conforming then how does use of this form influence what the poet is saying?
■ If the form has been changed in some way then you need to ask 'why?'

Rhythm methods

Just as poets can work with or against the tradition of the whole poem, they can do the same thing at the level of rhythms – which are just as much subject to the rules of tradition. One of the oldest rhythms in English poetry is known as iambic pentameter which was used by Chaucer in the fourteenth century and later by Shakespeare and Milton. Iambic pentameter consists of five stressed and unstressed beats per line of poetry, with the unstressed beat appearing first. Here is an example set out to emphasise the rhythm:

That TIME
of YEAR
thou MAY'ST
in ME
beHOLD
Shakespeare, *Sonnet 73*

The precise stress pattern can usually be worked out according to the natural stress of spoken English. If this causes any difficulty consider that 'behold' always has its stress on the second syllable rather than the first. Build your analysis around words of two or more syllables whose stress pattern should be obvious. If you need to practise this, try well-known catch-phrases such as, 'It's *good* to *talk*', or well-known names like, '*Will*iam *Shakes*peare' or '*Hump*ty-*Dump*ty'.

ACTIVITY 28

Rhythmic jousting: in a pair take it in turns to make up names that have the same rhythmic pattern. e.g. Tony Wilberforce – David Copperfield. You can vary the game according to your needs. Try making up a name that uses iambic pentameter.

ACTIVITY 29

Read the following extracts from well-known sonnets. Analyse the rhythm of each extract by marking stressed syllables with an accent and unstressed syllables with a cross. Then work out why the poet might have deviated from iambic pentameter in the context of the poem.

1 This extract comes from one of John Donne's *Holy Sonnets*, probably written in the early seventeenth century. In the poem the mood is predominantly passionate, with sexual metaphor expressing the poet's desire for God to take over his life.

Batter my heart, three-personed God; for, you
As yet but knock, breathe, shine, and seek to mend;

2 This extract is from Wordsworth's early nineteenth century lament for the world's materialism (an attitude that neglects spiritual values).

The world is too much with us; late and soon,
Getting and spending, we lay waste our powers:

3 Completely different in mood and rhythm, this is taken from Carol Ann Duffy's *Frau Freud* (1999), a light-hearted poke at the work of Sigmund Freud (see page 53). How does the rhythm help to express this?

Ladies, for argument's sake, let us say
that I've seen my fair share of ding-a-ling, member
and jock

COMMENTARY

Powerful sentiment is apparent in the first extract from the beginning. The stress in the first word 'batter' is on the first syllable and so the first line continues with a stressed/unstressed pattern. The second line departs even further from convention with its three consecutive stresses on 'knock', 'breathe' and 'shine'. The implication could be that he is such a sinner that God will have to try extra hard to get through to him. Wordsworth follows convention more strictly, especially in the first line. But in the second, the stress on the first syllables of 'getting' and 'spending' emphasises the world's determination to indulge in materialism. Duffy's sonnet is completely different in most respects. The light-hearted tone is reflected in the stress on every third syllable:

'LADies for ARGument's SAKE, let us SAY'
   1 2 3   1 2 3   1   2 3 1

which is sustained for most of the poem.

Analysis of rhythmic patterns has become less fashionable but it is still immensely useful, especially if you can find the moments in the poem when regularity is broken or when expectation is defeated. You will often find that those moments also hold something of thematic importance for comment.

A note on rhyme schemes. Traditionally, rhyme occurs at the end of each line of poetry. Critics have used letters of the alphabet to describe the pattern of rhymes throughout the poem. If, for example, the first line rhymes with the second, the third with the fourth, the fifth with the sixth, and so on, the rhyme scheme for this would be: aabbcc, etc. Try practising this by working out the scheme for a popular form such as the limerick – 'There was an old man from Ealing', etc.

ACTIVITY 30

Below is an example of a traditional Petrarchan sonnet (after the Italian poet, Petrarch 1304–1374) with a slight 'English' variation. Using the multi-choice questions that follow as cues, photocopy and annotate the poem to reveal the essentials of this form. Compare your answers with somebody else's. 'Answers' are given at the end of the chapter.

To Night

Mysterious Night! When our first parent knew
Thee from report divine, and heard thy name,
Did he not tremble for this lovely frame,
This glorious canopy of light and blue,
Yet 'neath a curtain of translucent dew,
Bathed in the rays of the great setting flame,
Hesperus with the host of heaven came,
And lo! Creation widened in man's view.
Who could have thought such darkness lay concealed
Within thy beams, O Sun! or who could find,
Whilst fly and leaf and insect stood revealed,
That to such countless orbs thou *mad'st* us blind!
Why do we then shun Death with anxious strife?
If Light can thus deceive, *wherefore* not Life?

Joseph Blanco White (1775–1841)

Hesperus: the Greek word for Venus, the evening star

mad'st: made

wherefore: why?

For each letter choose what, for you, is the best answer. Add your own preferred answers if you wish.

a The rhyme scheme divides the poem into the following unequal parts.
  1 four   **3** two
  2 three

b The argument of the poem divides into the following parts.
  1 three   **3** four
  2 two

c **1** The first eight lines are about the dangers of the night.
  2 They express regret for the loss of daylight.
  3 Night wasn't what it was expected to be.
  4 Night was perceived as a good thing to complement day.

d **1** The next four lines contradict what has just been said.
  2 They see things from another point of view.
  3 They express surprise.
  4 They express the mystery of creation.

e **1** The final couplet draws a conclusion from the previous twelve lines.
  2 It sums up what has been expressed already.
  3 It expresses the moral of the poem.
  4 It widens the subject of the poem.

f The argument of the poem goes like this:
  1 People were excited about the idea of night.
    When night came it did not disappoint.
    They knew their views were justified.
    So we should be excited about death.
  2 People were afraid of night.
    When it came it was like an invading army.
    Who would have believed it?
    So, death is always round the corner.
  3 People were afraid of night.
    But it was beautiful.
    Light can be deceptive.
    So, therefore, can life.

Getting a feel for the form

You have now established for yourself a set of expectations about sonnets and this can serve as a base line for further encounters with the form. But first you need to know a little more. You may have noticed that the first eight lines of the above sonnet rhyme in the pattern abba abba, comprising two quatrains (four line units). This Italian style then continued cdcdcd or cdecde. The problem for English poets who took up this style was that they had to produce four rhymes of each kind (for a and b) and this wasn't as easy in English as Italian. Thus the English sonnet was born in the sixteenth century with the pattern: abab cdcd efef gg. This final rhyming couplet was often an explicit moral tacked on to the end of the poem, something which would have been more popular then than now. According to Patterson (see reading list) Elizabethan sonnets that end with 'so', 'then' or 'therefore' signal an unsubtle ending that merely repeats an idea made obvious by the rest of the poem. Since then, several variations have emerged as the sonnet became fashionable once more. The popularity or not of the sonnet tells quite a lot about the style of poetry in vogue at a particular time; for example, it declined in popularity during the eighteenth century when the fashion was for longer narrative poems.

Sonnets were traditionally love poems by male poets. It was a way of demonstrating your skill as a poet as well as of winning your lady's heart. Often success at one was equated with success at the other. The Elizabethans (such as Shakespeare) used the sonnet as a way of developing an argument. Love then became a vehicle for writing about some other concept such as: time, eternity, death, etc. After Shakespeare many poets wrote directly about these ideas.

Here are some of the essential features of the form:

- There is usually a 'turn' at the end of the 'octave' (the first eight lines). This means that there is a change or development in the poet's thought. The rhyme scheme of the English form tended to obscure this a little – because of the three groups of four – but it is usually still apparent.
- The last six lines will tend to solve a problem set up in the first eight.
- Sonnets are usually tightly woven structures that try to achieve an overall 'unity' – in the same way that a painting has an overall design, pattern or shape.
- Sonnets are supposed to bear a natural relationship to human thought and to other naturally occurring patterns. The ratio of eight lines to six reflects a ratio called the golden section, which is also apparent in, for example, the design of a snail's shell. Visually sonnets are also close to being squares. These factors may account for the satisfaction afforded by the form.
- Sonnets often take the form of an argument or extended metaphor.
- There should be a sense of inevitability about the development of ideas in a sonnet.

ACTIVITY 31

Test your sense of the inevitable in a sonnet by considering the two lines below. Was the couplet at the end of *To Night* the original or is it the one below? Discuss your views with a partner, gathering evidence from the whole of the above section on the sonnet. Answer at the end of the chapter.

> Why do we then meet dark with hideous fight?
> If light can thus deceive, can we know right?

ACTIVITY 32

Key Skills: Communication – reading

Use the information under 'getting a feel for the form' to read the poem *In the Park* below and compare it with *To Night*. These questions are for guidance:

- Is there an argument in the poem?
- Can you paraphrase the poem's logic as in question 'F' above?

- How has Gwen Harwood adhered to or adapted a traditional sonnet form to suit her purposes?
- How are your responses affected by the differences in form?

In the Park

She sits in the park. Her clothes are out of date.
Two children whine and bicker, tug her skirt.
A third draws aimless patterns in the dirt.
Someone she loved once passes by – too late

'but for the grace of God . . .' – an expression completed by the words 'go I' and meaning 'that could have been me, but thank God . . .'

To feign indifference to that casual nod.
'How nice,' et cetera. 'Time holds great surprises.'
From his neat head unquestionably rises
a small balloon . . . 'but for the grace of God . . .'

They stand a while in flickering light, rehearsing
the children's names and birthdays. 'It's so sweet
to hear their chatter, watch them grow and thrive,'
she says to his departing smile. Then, nursing
the youngest child, sits staring at her feet.
To the wind she says, 'They have eaten me alive.'

Gwen Harwood, *Selected Poems*, 1975

COMMENTARY Here are some ideas that you may have built your thinking around. Harwood depicts a situation in the poem rather than presenting a thought or idea directly as does *To Night*. She builds on the tradition of the significant moment rather than the extended metaphor and therefore doesn't require such intense logic as *To Night*. The content is also perhaps typically twentieth century in that the significant moment is a depressing one. The rhyme is closer to the original Italian than *To Night*, a fact which may surprise given the informality of the language and the 'rough edges' such as the incomplete fragment 'but for the grace of God . . .' The first quatrain also overlaps neatly with the second so that the words 'too late' show both her feelings about the past and how she is reacting in the present. The question of a 'turn' is less easily resolved. The passing of time in 'They stand a while . . .' suggests movement to another phase but how that phase is to be described is unclear. There is a sense of inevitability, given the description of the woman in the first quatrain, yet that final plea (?) is far from predictable.

Extension activities

ACTIVITY 33

Does Shakespeare's *Sonnet 130* ('Shall I compare thee to a summer's day?') live up to the following claim? 'He achieves originality within a rather exhausted and cliché-ridden traditional form, and this is ultimately a fine compliment to his mistress in that she is the inspiration for this originality; he flatters by not seeming to.' (Peet and Robinson, 1977)

ACTIVITY 34

If you are studying sonnets, try to re-write the last two lines of one of them. Can you write the lines so that they follow the logic and form of the poem as well as copy its rhythm?

ACTIVITY 35

Compare Shakespeare's *Sonnet 18* and Elizabeth Barrett Browning's *Sonnet 43* with respect to the following: The way that the poems are structured in their use of repetition, rhyme scheme and the structure of the 'logic' behind the poem. Carry out a full response in the light of these differences.

ACTIVITY 36

Re-write the sextet of *In the Park* so that it ends with a rhyming couplet and states its 'moral' explicitly.

> **Does the form of a poem really matter or do we just like to think it does?**

Fabliau: Chaucer's dirty tricks

There is a tendency to think that the older the literature you are studying the less chance you as a student have of considering and developing alternative ways of reading it. Surely after all these years the critics have made up their minds? The answer to this is 'no', and it will continue to be 'no' as long as new ways of thinking about the meanings of poems continue to evolve. In fact, Chaucer's *Canterbury Tales* seem to be written in a way that invites more than one interpretation.

The *Canterbury Tales* were written between the late 1380s and Chaucer's death in 1400. They comprise about twenty-five tales (the work was unfinished) told by a group of pilgrims on their way to visit the bones of St Thomas à Becket at Canterbury. A number of factors combine to suggest to the modern reader that the tales can be read in a variety of ways:

- Chaucer presents a variety of points of view through his contrasting characters
- He undermines his own storytellers
- The characters behave inconsistently, thus casting doubt on what they say
- Chaucer sometimes invites the reader to interpret the tale
- The tales were unfinished, so increasing speculation as to how to fill the gaps.

Fab expectations

The following four fragments tell a little of the stories of four of Chaucer's tales. Put these tales into two categories and describe your reasons for this categorisation.

The Shipman's Tale: involves a lovers' triangle between a merchant, his wife and a monk. Whilst the merchant is away the wife tells the monk that she needs 100 francs and that her husband does not satisfy her in bed. The monk borrows the 100 francs from the merchant, gives it to the wife and has sex with her in return . . .

The Knight's Tale: Emily is loved by two knights – Palamon and Arcite – who are cousins and friends. The two fight for Emily's hand. Arcite wins but is thrown from his horse and killed.

Before he dies he recommends that Palamon should marry Emily. The two marry in bliss.

The Franklin's Tale: a knight and his lady are deeply in love but whilst the knight is away another highly accomplished young man declares his love for the lady. She promises him love if he can remove all of the rocks from the coast. This he accomplishes but is so aggrieved at the sorrow he has caused both knight and lady that he refuses to accept her . . .

The Merchant's Tale: is about January, a jealous old husband who, for the satisfaction of his lust, takes a young wife who deceives him after he has gone blind. As a result of the wife's clever deceptions, January ends up deliriously happy.

Here we will consider just one way of thinking about the tales, namely with respect to genre. Chaucer used at least two genres in telling his stories: romance and fabliau. The **romance** was intended to provide examples of such noble virtues as courtly love and chivalry. The **fabliau**, by contrast, overturns these values by showing us, in a humorous way, the ugly under-belly of human behaviour. In the above activity the Shipman's and the Merchant's tales are fabliaux whereas the other two tales are romances. However, as you may have guessed by now, these genres are never 'pure' and the ways in which they deviate from purity can help us to interpret the stories. The rest of this chapter will focus on what to expect from fabliaux.

Key Skills: Communication – discussion/presentation

You will already be familiar with the plot motif – a kind of set piece – of the girl with two lovers. In a small group, predict how a fabliau, or any comical genre, might develop this situation into a story. Use some of the ideas in the above plot summaries. How might you develop a moral out of what happens?

Here is an example of a fabliau in summary form that shows many of the characteristics of the genre:

Heile arranges to let three men visit her at different times on one night. While she is in bed with the miller, the priest comes. She sends the miller to hide in a tub in the rafters. While she is in bed with the priest, the miller overhears the priest talking about the Flood. When the blacksmith comes and knocks at the door, begging at least to kiss her, she persuades the priest to stick his bottom out of the window. The blacksmith, having kissed it, returns with a hot iron and, in a repeat of the window-scene, burns the priest, whose cries for water cause the miller to cut himself loose and fall from the rafters. The moral is that injury and shame come to those who consort with whores.

Bryan and Dempster, *Source and Analogues of Chaucer's Canterbury Tales*, in Helen Phillips, *An Introduction to the Canterbury Tales: Reading, Fiction and Context*

ACTIVITY 39

Here is a series of statements about Chaucer's fabliaux. Which ones apply to the story summary above? There are 'answers' at the end of the chapter.

1 They enter a world where normal morals, normal sanctions and normal consequences are removed.
2 They provide models for appropriate behaviour.
3 They involve ingenious strategies and bizarrely unexpected outcomes.
4 Plots are highly artificial and symmetrical.
5 They involve conflict of ideals or beliefs.
6 They involve ordinary characters rather than high-born or noble ones.
7 There is a serious message to be taken from the story.
8 They promote positive images of women.
9 They make men look stupid.

A summary of the Miller's Tale

Chaucer's *Miller's Tale* involves four main characters: an old carpenter and his young wife, Alison, a student lodger Nicholas and Absalon, a parish clerk. The latter two compete for Alison's affections and the story climaxes when Nicholas tricks the carpenter into believing that he must prepare for an imminent flood. Whilst the carpenter waits for the Flood in his bathtub in the attic, Nicholas has his way with Alison. Meanwhile, Absalon begs for a kiss at the window. Nicholas gets Alison to thrust her back-side from the window and when Absalon realises what he has kissed, he borrows a branding iron from a local blacksmith. Returning to the window he again begs a kiss and this time Nicholas puts out his back-side, delivering a thunderous fart. However, Absalon thrusts in the iron, Nicholas shouts for water and the Carpenter, thinking that the end of the world is up, releases his bathtub and plunges to the ground.

ACTIVITY 40

1 Compare the summary of the *Miller's Tale* above with the story of Heile (page 37). How does Chaucer deviate from this traditional fabliau? How are these differences likely to change your reactions to the story?
2 Read the ending given below. Respond to it in as much detail as you can, given the issues that will already have arisen. You might like to consider: issues of punishment for wrong-doings; the extent to which the story closes off speculation; gender. To what extent does the whole tale meet the expectations raised by the fabliau (Heile) summarised above? How might you alter your views on fabliaux as established in activity 39?

The Miller's End

The carpenter has just been exposed by Alison and Nicholas as a madman for making them keep tubs in the attic in preparation for Noah's flood. Below are the last few lines of the *Miller's Tale* in the original Middle English. Using the glossary you should be able to make sense of them:

wight – bloke *swyved* – a crude term for sexual intercourse (f-word); *hir nether ye* – lower eye *towte* – bum *rowte* – crowd.

And every *wight* gan laughen at this stryf.
Thus *swyved* was this carpenteris wyf,
For al his kepyng and his jalousye,
And Absalon hath kist *hir nether ye*,
And Nicholas is scalded in the *towte*.
. . . and God save al the *rowte*!

ACTIVITY 41

Key Skills: Communication – reading; IT – different sources

A great deal of twentieth century poetry is written in free verse and seems to express completely original ideas. But don't be deceived. Most poets are aware of the forms and themes that have gone before and may be consciously using them. For example, how is your reading of Duffy's poem *Mean Time* influenced when you look at it alongside Auden's *Funeral Blues*? Using some of the poetry you are studying for your course, do some research into relevant poetry that preceded it. Then look more closely at the relationship between the two. Here are some examples:

Poet being studied	Relevant precedents?
Ted Hughes	Nature poets, especially the nineteenth century Romantics.
W. H. Auden	Traditional ballads.
Seamus Heaney	The Romantics but especially Wordsworth's use of his childhood as subject matter.
Carol Ann Duffy	Robert Browning – use of the dramatic monologue.

Key Skills: the following activities could be developed to meet several key skills

ACTIVITY 42

Explore the gender of the writer and the recipient of the poem. You will need to do some research using encyclopedias. How, for example, did Elizabeth Barrett Browning develop the sonnet, considering that she was a woman writing to a man? What do Duffy's love poems do to the tradition of love poetry?

ACTIVITY 43

An important context for the *Canterbury Tales* is the connection between the individual tales. If you are studying a fabliau or a romance (see activity 37), read summaries of examples of both types. Use a translation such as the one by Neville Coghill or the BBC videos (available from BBC Education) to get a quick impression. Then consider such questions as: how many of the traditional elements of fabliaux does Chaucer use? Why does he change some of them in the context of some of the other tales? How does he make use of contrasts between fabliau and romance?

ACTIVITY 44

Carry out an extended study of a particular form of poetry such as the 'carpe diem' poem which urges readers to 'seize the day' – in other words to combat the onward march of time by living for the present. Poems to get you started might be: Andrew Marvell's – *To His Coy Mistress*; Robert Herrick's – *To the Virgins, to Make Much of Time*; Robert Graves's – *Sick Love*; A. E. Housman's – *Loveliest of Trees*. A website containing many poems and search facilities can be found at: http://www.bartleby.com/verse/.

ACTIVITY 45

John Donne's *The Sun Rising* (see page 80) is an example of a form of poetry called an **aubade**. An aubade is usually a love poem from lover to loved one at the break of day. An obvious point of comparison with Donne is the dialogue between Romeo and Juliet after their first night of love when they discuss whether they can hear the lark or the nightingale. This scene might have influenced Donne as he was writing at around the same time as Shakespeare. Aubades with a difference were also written in the twentieth century by William Empsom, Louis MacNeice and Philip Larkin; all were called simply *Aubade*. Research the ways in which poets have used the aubade form.

ACTIVITY 46

Examine the similarities between Emily Dickinson's *It was not death, for I stood up* (page 54) and the riddle form. In what ways is this form appropriate to the subject of the poem?

ACTIVITY 47

Some critics say that nature poetry is dead. Using a sample of the work of two nature poets that you are studying, examine the ways in which they each use nature for their own purposes. You are likely to need to refer to the Romantics for this. Other nature poets might include: Edward Thomas, Robert Frost, Ted Hughes, R. S. Thomas, Seamus Heaney. For further guidance on comparing texts see *Linking Texts*, Jackie Baker, Hodder and Stoughton, 2001.

Summary

This chapter has looked at the genres or forms of poetry, emphasising two aspects: that forms change over time in important ways; that forms create expectations in the reader. Examples of different sonnet forms and variations on the fabliaux have been used to illustrate these ideas.

Answers to activity 30 (page 32): A – 2 or 3; B – 4; C – 3 or 4; D – 3; E – 1, 2 and 4; F – 3.

Answer to activity 31 (page 34): The couplet at the end of the poem is the original.

Answers to activity 39 (page 38): 1 True **2** True **3** True **4** True **5** False **6** True **7** True **8** False **9** True

Further Reading

Gail Ashton, *Studying Chaucer: Approaching the Canterbury Tales*, Studymates, 2000. This is excellently pitched for study at AS level and, unlike many study guides, offers alternatives without spoon-feeding 'answers'.

Glynn Austen, 'The Reeve's Tale and its Audience' in *The English Review*, Vol 11, No 2, Nov 2000. Considers interesting variations on the fabliau.

Caroline Cole, 'The Miller vs The Knight', in *The English Review*, Vol 11, No 1, September 2000. A demanding read but useful for comparing romance and fabliau.

John Hines, *The Fabliau in English*, Longman, 1993. A detailed study of the genre. Accessible to students in part.

Don Paterson, *101 Sonnets*, Faber and Faber, 1999. An invaluable collection that covers a wide range of sonnets with a useful if brief commentary.

www.sonnets.org – an accessible and comprehensive sonnet web-site with time-line and criticism.

http://cwolf.uaa.alaska.edu/~afdtk/ECT_Main.htm. *The Electronic Chaucer* contains just about everything and more. Could seriously damage your phone bill.

4 Social Criticism

Poetry, though remote from life, enhances life's values.

Valentile

We touch under glaze,
hands fused in the firing.
Two clays baked as one.

The idea of work is important	

Social criticism in action

In this poem romantic love, and the bonding that it entails, is a metaphor for the poet's views on manual work. Here physical work is praised as if the poet were in love with it, hence 'valentine' becomes 'valentile'. The work of the tiler is chosen because the tiler creates something using the most basic ingredients and processes: 'clay' and 'firing', and so his work stands for the creation of artefacts from natural materials. The end result is the unifying effect that this act of creation has on the people involved. 'Hands' carry out the work, with 'fused' emphasising the unity they achieve by working together in the firing. The fact that there are two 'clays' at the end (and not 'tiles') suggests that not only does work unite people but it is also a constant reminder that all humans are mortal.

The idea of work is important

Manual work is often the focus

Emphasises the effect of work on people

By praising 'work' the poem is seen as a progressive text (see page 43)

Refers to use of language

Usually some attitude towards work is expressed

Points out what is associated with labour

Like the feminist approach to criticism, social approaches assume that there is something wrong with society. Feminists feel that women have been given a rough deal by society and that poetry must reflect that situation. In the same way a social approach can focus on just about anyone else who might have been pushed to the edge of society: the working class and ethnic minority groups, for example. Not many works of literature can escape this approach: 'Pierre Bruno, a lecturer at Dijon University, has applied Marxist analysis to the text [*Harry Potter*] and concluded that the four houses at Hogwarts School represent competing social groups . . .' (*The Week*, Feb, 2001).

This kind of criticism has often been associated with Marxism – the theory underlying communism – but such a narrow way of seeing the social approach is not helpful at this level. It is best seen in terms of any aspect of society that can productively be applied to a poem. This chapter will focus briefly on social class and race.

Aspects of social criticism

- The representation of a particular social class.
- Showing how one social class has taken advantage of another.
- The decline of an aspect of a country – certain values or 'culture'.
- Issues of power between, for example, religious groups.
- The position in society of certain social groups: immigrants, homosexuals, etc.

Marxist literary criticism

Karl Marx (1819–1883) was the philosopher behind communism, the political system that emphasised equality and joint ownership in the countries of Eastern Europe and the Russian Empire, for example, until around 1990. This was, for many years, the most important kind of social criticism, but it has declined in importance since the collapse of the Russian Empire (the USSR).

Taking on this theory in its entirety at this stage is rather unnecessary baggage that is likely to get in the way of both the poem and your response to it. It's best to take what you can from Marxism and use it to enhance your own ideas. A useful starting point is to consider whether or not a poem or a collection promotes equality in society or not.

If a poem promotes equality it is called **progressive**. If a poem does not promote equality it is called **non-progressive**. Progressive texts will often be explicitly about social class, just as feminists often write about women and their position in society. As Marxist societies tended to support the lot of the ordinary working person, such poems will praise manual labour (as in the analysis of *Valentile* above) or suggest the dignity that can arise from absorption in menial work. On the other hand, they might also expose the dangers of repetitive or unengaging work, exposing the bosses whose power keeps the workers in their lowly position.

Non-progressive texts are often more difficult to spot. Because they are non-progressive they are often about nothing connected with the working class, politics, economics, power, etc – so it would seem. If, for example, the poem is about love it might simply take for granted that society:

- exploits the poor for the benefit of the rich
- is divided into various social classes
- is built around the family unit and capitalism.

And because it takes these things for granted, Marxists assume that it supports them.

When analysing a poem it is useful to describe what the poem values or praises as being at the centre. What the poem does not value is at the margin (see the diagram below). *La Belle Dame Sans Merci* (page 65) is clearly not in any obvious way about society, so is it a non-progressive text? You are advised to familiarise yourself with the poem now if you have not already done so.

The knight is presented at the centre (readers experience his point of view) and the lady is at the margins of society. The knight is alone but is not expected to be (in line 2) so he is usually considered a part of society. Later he is associated with rulers and their servants: kings, princes and warriors (stanza 10). The lady, on the other hand, is 'wild', she speaks in 'language strange' and she is a 'faery's child' (clearly, this approach would also support a feminist reading of the poem). A simple diagram might help to clarify this social reading:

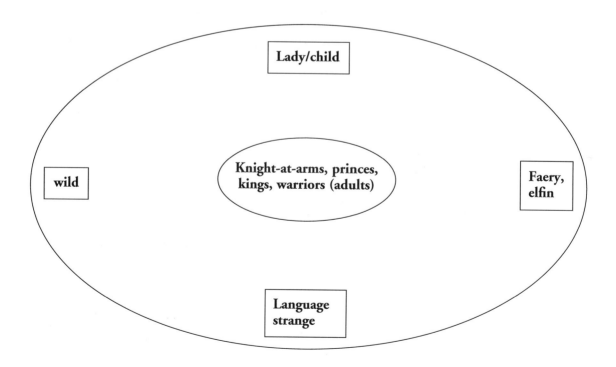

This paints a picture of a society with those in charge at the centre and the woman marginalised because of the language she speaks, because she is beyond control and is identified as coming from an unreal place. As a result of the knight's interaction with the lady, he too has been banished to the margins – to 'the cold hill side'. This brief account of the poem forms the basis of a social reading.

ACTIVITY 48

Key Skills: Communication – discussion

Discuss with a partner whether or not you would consider *La Belle Dame Sans Merci* to be a progressive or non-progressive text. In other words does it offer approval of the 'society' described in the above diagram or is it critical of it?

COMMENTARY

At first *La Belle Dame Sans Merci* appears to be a non-progressive text. It is not apparently about equality in society but rather seems to tell the story of a knight who has been the victim of a misunderstanding. If the poem sets up the society described in the diagram above it does not appear to be critical of it. On the contrary, it seems to suggest that the knight, his power and the things he stands for at the centre of the poem are in danger from those at the margins, and the sympathy that is drawn for him suggests that this must not be allowed to happen. On the other hand it could be taken to suggest that whatever the knight stands for is lost – that he and the power he is associated with must topple. Thus you could argue that it is a progressive text in that it foresees the breakdown of the society in the above diagram.

ACTIVITY 49

Key Skills – IT – present information

Imagine that you are storyboarding a short film based on *La Belle Dame Sans Merci*. Produce two versions: one for a communist audience – for the Cuban government, for example; and one for a Western capitalist audience. Show how the poem can be interpreted in two different ways. How far do you have to depart from the original poem for either interpretation? Which do you feel is more 'true' to the original poem?

ACTIVITY 50

Before you read the poems below by D. H. Lawrence (1885–1930) brainstorm associations for *opera* and *labourers*. Read and respond to the two poems. Then read the poems in terms of social class, paying attention to:

■ images associated with the labourers

■ images associated with reactions to opera in the first two stanzas of the second poem
■ the image of the barman in the last stanza
■ the speaker's reaction to what he sees.

Would you consider these poems to be progressive or non-progressive texts?

Morning Work

A gang of labourers on the piled wet timber
That shines blood-red beside the railway siding
Seem to be making out of the blue of the morning
Something faery and fine, the shuttles sliding,

The red-gold spools of their hands and their faces swinging
Hither and thither across the high crystalline frame
Of day: trolls at the cave of ringing cerulean mining
And laughing with labour, living their work like a game.

After the Opera

Down the stone stairs
Girls with their large eyes wide with tragedy
Lift looks of shocked and momentous emotion up at me . . .
And I smile.

Ladies
Stepping like birds with their bright and pointed feet
Peer anxiously forth, as if for a boat to carry them out of the wreckage;
And among the wreck of the theatre crowd

I stand and smile.
They take tragedy so becomingly;
Which pleases me.

But when I meet the weary eyes
The reddened, aching eyes of the bar-man with thin arms,
I am glad to go back where I came from.

Race: reading from the margins

Readings that emphasise race usually focus on power relationships between the races, in a similar way to feminism's concern with men and women. Not surprisingly, such criticism describes the oppression of the black races by the dominant whites but, in theory, it can deal with the relationship between any two races. In a more general sense this kind of reading asks the question: how would certain racial groups read this poem?

It can be used in two ways:

1 To read poetry explicitly about racial issues, such as poetry by Afro-Caribbeans: Grace Nichols, Derek Walcott, Benjamin Zephaniah, James Berry, Merle Hodge, Kamu Braithwaite, etc.
2 To read poetry that is not explicitly about race but refers to race sufficiently to warrant criticism. This is called 'reading against the grain' and it is practised in much the same way that feminists read against the grain (see page 79).

What to look for when reading like this:

1 Ideas concerning what is at the centre of things (or important) and what is at the margin (unimportant or rejected). This can be represented by drawing a circle as in the example above (on page 44) or by using two columns, one entitled 'at the centre', the other 'at the margin' (as in the example on page 48)

2 Images of blackness or whiteness. What are these things associated with in a poem?

3 Attitudes explicitly expressed towards racial issues or racial stereotypes.

ACTIVITY 51

Using the idea of a 'centre' and a 'margin', analyse, in a broad way, the historical relationship between black and white people, putting your evidence at appropriate places on a diagram. You might include evidence such as slavery and South Africa.

ACTIVITY 52

Read and respond to the poem below by Grace Nichols from *The Fat Black Woman's Poems* and then use points 1 to 3 above to guide your reading. Look up 'steatopygous' in a good dictionary.

Thoughts drifting through the Fat Black Woman's head while having a full bubble bath

Steatopygous sky
Steatopygous sea
Steatopygous waves
Steatopygous me

O how I long to place my foot
on the head of *anthropology*

anthropology – a branch of sociology that compares societies, particularly traditional or developing ones

to swing my breasts
in the face of history
to scrub my back
with the dogma of *theology*

theology – the study of religion.

to put my soap
in the slimming industry's
profitsome spoke

Steatopygous sky
Steatopygous sea
Steatopygous waves
Steatopygous me

COMMENTARY

At the centre of the poem	At the margin of the poem
All things 'steatopygous'	
My foot	The head of anthropology
My breasts	The face of history
My back	The dogma of theology
My soap	The slimming industry's profitsome spoke

The poet has structured the poem so that almost all of the things at the centre are to do with parts of the body. Along with the title of the collection, *The Fat Black Woman's Poems*, this seems to emphasise the poet's reclaiming of her body as her own. Notice how the repetition of 'my' makes all of these references personal in contrast to the coldness of 'the', which introduces everything at the margin. The word 'steatopygous' takes the references to the body into a political context as the activity below will reveal. Notice that everything at the margin is traditionally powerful: academic study and big business. How does this centre and margin compare with the one you suggested in Activity 51?

> **Can this method only really be used with poems that are about black and other ethnic groups?**

ACTIVITY 53

In the extract that follows, the critic, Jan Montefiore, is discussing the above poem. The Fat Black Woman is not Nichols herself but a caricature who uses humour to redefine the way that 'blackness', 'fatness' and 'being a woman' are perceived.

1 What evidence does Montefiore provide to back up her arguments about irony and humour?
2 Do you think this critic is writing primarily about race or gender?

The comic possibilities of her *redefinitions* are at their finest in the contemplative poem *Thoughts drifting through the fat black woman's head while having a full bubble bath* ... The refrain identifies the Fat Black Woman's opulent curves with the brightness and wide horizons of a Caribbean seascape: sky, sea and waves. The theme is similar to the poem *Beauty* which invokes the Fat Black Woman drifting in the sea while a wave turns over 'to hug her shape', except that here the means of self-assertion is comic. 'Steatopygous' means 'fat-buttocked', which makes the refrain a nonsense rhyme, partly because its adjective-noun combinations make grammatical but not literal sense (seas, skies and waves do not have bodies) and partly because of the contrast of registers between the three-times repeated, polysyllabic, Greek-derived 'scientific' adjective and the monosyllabic, down-to-earth nouns which it qualifies.

There is a particularly delicious irony in the Fat Black Woman choosing the adjective 'steatopygous' to celebrate the beauty of herself and her race in that this word has a history of deeply unpleasant racist and sexist definition. The *Oxford English Dictionary* defines 'steatopygia' from which the adjective is derived, as 'A protuberance of the buttocks, due to an abnormal accumulation of fat in and behind the hips and thighs, found (more markedly on women than men) as a racial characteristic of certain peoples, esp. the Hottentot Bushmen of South Africa'; each of its illustrative quotations uses the word to ascribe a 'racial deformity' to African people – principally women. Furthermore, as Sander Gilman has shown in an important essay on the 'Hottentot Venus' steatopygia was used symbolically to associate the African woman with animals and prostitutes as a subhuman, over-sexed source of pollution. No wonder that the Fat Black Woman desires to make the master discourse of abstract thought her washpot: anthropology is answerable for racist definitions of Africans; history has traditionally excluded African people; theology has held women and black people accursed as 'daughters of Eve'... and the slimming industry squeezes women into a 'profitsome' stereotype; and she would like to squash them all with her massive and weighty self.

Jan Montefiore, *Feminism and Poetry*

redefinitions – ethnic and other groups often seek to redefine themselves in a positive light in their work. Perhaps the most famous redefinition is of the word 'queer' by gay writers.

COMMENTARY

Much of Montefiore's evidence for the humour surrounding 'steatopygous' is linguistic, with the references to registers, adjectives and monosyllables. But she also cites the *Oxford English Dictionary* (not to be overlooked when studying poetry) as evidence for the way in which 'steatopygous' has traditionally been used, as well as the work of Sander Gilman. This is wide-ranging evidence that enhances the status of the criticism. As for the question of the main focus in this text – gender or race? – the feminist angle and the racial angle are clearly closely linked here. The idea of a woman re-defining her body is perhaps foremost but it is dependent on the racial stereotype which has arguably been the more powerful historical influence.

ACTIVITY 54

John Donne's poem *The Sun Rising* (page 80) appears to be about a couple waking up in the morning and declaring their love. But it could also be read 'from the margins' as a poem with racial or political overtones. Using the ideas on page 44 to help you, is it possible to read the poem in this way?

ACTIVITY 55

A leading critic of the day, Francis Jeffrey, found Wordsworth's contributions to *Lyrical Ballads* (1798) to be subversive in the sense that they threatened to destabilise society. Jeffrey had two main reasons for thinking this: Wordsworth, in his introduction to the collection, had written of the importance of using ordinary language in poetry; secondly, England was at war with France when the collection was published and so many people feared revolt from within. Explore the themes and language of Wordworth's poetry with reference to this opinion.

ACTIVITY 56

Key Skills – various

The Romantic poets wrote at a time of great social upheaval – the expansion of the British Empire and the establishment of modern industrial society. Referring to one or more of these poets that you are studying (Blake, Wordsworth, Coleridge, Keats, Shelley, Byron), try applying the ideas of the centre and the margin or progressive and non-progressive texts to a selection of their work.

Summary

This chapter has considered two types of social criticism: Marxism and the perspective of racial groups, sometimes called post-colonial criticism. It has used the visual analogy of 'reading from the centre' and 'reading from the margins'.

Further Reading

Alison Donnell and Sarah Lawson Welsh, *The Routledge Reader in Caribbean Literature*, Routledge, 1996. A vast resource of readings, poems and prose extracts.

Amon Saba Saakana, *The Colonial Legacy in Caribbean Literature*, Karnak House, 1987. Useful background for teachers.

Ramon Selden, *Practising Theory and Reading Literature – an Introduction*, Harvester Wheatsheaf, 1989. Plenty of practical examples here although some are demanding.

Wasafiri – Caribbean, African, Asian and Associated Literatures in English, Turnaround Publisher Services Ltd, Unit 3, Olympia Trading Estate, Coburg Road, Wood Green, London. http://www.qmw.ac.uk/~english/publications/Wasafiri.html A journal providing useful cultural background and theory.

5 Digging up the Dirt: Psychological and Psychoanalytic Criticism

Every work of art stems from a wound in the soul of the artist . . . All her [Sylvia Plath's] creative work tells just one story: her Oedipal love for her father, her complex relationship with her mother, the attempt at suicide, the shock therapy.

Ted Hughes, The *Independent on Sunday*, Nov 1998

Valentile

We touch under glaze,
hands fused in the firing.
Two clays baked as one.

Psychological criticism in action

Straight to the underlying ideas

This is a poem about sex and death. It is disguised as a love poem and the word-play on 'valentine' also distracts readers from these darker meanings. 'Tiles' are put on the surface of things but this poem secretly celebrates what goes on underneath, hence 'under glaze'. Interestingly, if you take the 'l' out of 'glaze' you get 'gaze', so again the 'l' plays a part in hiding the poet's true feelings; he secretly wants to expose his desire to the 'gaze' of others. The second line obviously refers to sexual intercourse, with 'fused' suggesting a physical joining and the intensity of passion. Again the true nature of this passion is concealed in the alliteration on the 'f' with 'fire': what the poet really wants to say is 'fuck'. The final line hides behind the suggested cliché 'two

This type of reading often looks for symbols

Desires are often important

Sex sometimes features in this kind of reading

Reference to language

hearts beat as one' but again its purpose is much
darker. 'Clay', by association with 'earth', ◄————
suggests 'death'; such is the intensity of the
passion that the poet sees it as final. In other
words the poet can see nothing in life as intense
as this 'fire', so it is like a death, total obliteration
of the self.

> *Taboo subjects like death feature strongly*

> *Another symbol*

Many people think that psychoanalysis is a theory that relates everything to sex. This is partly true – sex often rears its head but only because it seems to be behind what we know as unconscious desires. Understanding this approach means grasping a few basic psychological concepts that can be used over and over again and lead you towards genuinely new, if sometimes controversial, interpretations.

This approach to analysing poetry has taken three forms during the hundred years of its existence. The main focus can be on:

Writer	**Text**	**Reader**
Analysis of the psychology of the writer in connection with the poems	Analysis of the psychology of the characters and images in the poems	Analysis of the psychology of the reader

ACTIVITY 57

Key Skills: Communication – discussion

What do you think would be the advantages and disadvantages of each of these approaches?

Which do you prefer? Discuss this in a small group.

COMMENTARY

Psychological criticism often tends to require biographical information about the poet, so that it can tend, if you are not too careful, to move away from the text under discussion, which might only provide one or two bits of evidence for or against a particular psychological reading. Emphasising the psychology of the reader has certainly been attempted by some critics. But again this approach tends to take us away from the text and you are unlikely, for A level, to have time to consider individual readers. What might be useful is to consider the psychology of particular kinds of readers; for example, the psychology of readers at a particular period of history may explain the way that a particular poem was read. Clearly, for psychological criticism to work the focus must remain predominantly on the poem itself.

This chapter will introduce the middle of the above approaches, although we will inevitably also be drawn into discussion of the poets themselves.

It should be fairly obvious that psychological criticism attempts to uncover the psychology behind a poem or, sometimes, of the poet behind a series of poems. A word of caution about two confusable terms: 'psychoanalysis' refers specifically to the work of Sigmund Freud and any criticism called psychoanalytic will use Freudian symbolism. 'Psychological' is a much broader term that can be applied to a range of approaches; here it will be used loosely to mean underlying mental processes, states and conflicts in the poem.

Psychoanalysis started with Sigmund Freud at around the turn of the nineteenth century. Freud believed that much human behaviour could be explained with reference to unconscious desires that go back to childhood experiences. For an amusing introduction to Freud from an interesting point of view, try reading Carol Ann Duffy's poem, *Frau Freud* in her collection *The World's Wife* (see page 31).

If the meaning of a poem is unconscious and so cannot be observed, how can you ever argue against it?

When to use psychological reading

It is difficult to give a precise answer to this question but watch out for poems about:

- the poet or a persona's feelings towards other people
- relationships between children and parents
- obsessions and 'hang-ups'
- fears
- relationships between men and women
- when there is a suppressed or hidden feeling regarding a taboo subject.

An obvious occasion to use a psychological approach is when the poet is known to have had psychological problems and you are likely to become aware of aspects of the poet's life fairly quickly after reading some of the poems. Examples of so-called 'confessional' poetry have been written by Sylvia Plath (1932–1963) and Emily Dickinson (1830–1886). In these cases you might regard reading the poem as filling in the gap between the biography and the poems, based on your reading of both. But don't allow yourself to be swamped by the interpretation that often goes with biography. Your psychological approach to the poems should work something like this:

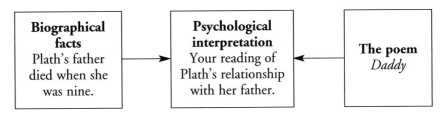

ACTIVITY 58

Below is an extract from a short biography about Emily Dickinson and following it is a poem by Dickinson. Using both the poem and the hints provided in the biography, suggest what kind of psychological experience lies between the biography and the poem.

> . . . during her early years she was lively, witty and sociable, but from her mid-twenties she gradually withdrew into an inner world, eventually, in her forties, refusing to leave her home, and avoiding all contact with strangers, although she maintained intimate correspondences with people she never saw face to face. Her emotional life remains mysterious, despite much speculation about a possible disappointed love affair . . .'

M. Drabble, *Oxford Companion to English Literature*

It was not Death, for I stood up

It was not Death, for I stood up,
And all the Dead, lie down –
It was not Night, for all the Bells
Put out their tongues, for Noon.

It was not Frost, for on my Flesh
I felt *Siroccos* – crawl –
Nor Fire – for just my Marble feel
Could keep a *Chancel*, cool –

And yet, it tasted, like them all,
The Figures I have seen
Set orderly, for Burial,
Reminded me, of mine –

As if my life were shaven,
And fitted to a frame,
And could not breathe without a key,
And 'twas like Midnight, some –

When everything that ticked – has stopped –
And space stares all around –
Or grisly frosts – first Autumn morns,
Repeal the Beating Ground –

But, most, like Chaos – Stopless – cool –
Without a Chance, or *Spar* –
Or even a Report of Land –
To justify – Despair.

Siroccos – hot winds from Africa

Chancel – an area of a church near the altar

Repeal – cancel

Spar – a beam as part of a ship's rigging

Symbolism

Reference to symbols is not, of course, unique to psychological reading, but symbolism is included here as an introduction to ideas underlying the images that can often be found in poetry. Here is Ted Hughes on the power of symbols to allow alternative interpretations:

A jaguar after all can be received in several different aspects ... he is a beautiful, powerful nature spirit, he is a homicidal maniac, he is a supercharged piece of cosmic machinery, he is a symbol of man's baser nature shoved down into the id and growing cannibal murderous with deprivation, he is an ancient symbol of Dionysus since he is a leopard raised to the ninth power, he is a precise historical symbol to the bloody-minded Aztecs and so on. Or he is simply a demon ... a lump of ectoplasm. A lump of astral energy ...

The symbol opens all these things ... it is the reader's own nature that selects.

ed. Dyson. Quoted in *Casebook*, Orig. published in Ekbert Faas, *Ted Hughes: The Unaccommodated Universe.*

Psychological interpretation often revolves around symbols – objects, images or actions that stand for important concepts in a poem. Freud developed his system of symbols by analysing the dreams of his patients, but many of his symbols can also be found in the mythology of several different cultures. Note that a symbol isn't quite the same thing as an image in poetry. Imagery appeals to the senses, usually the visual, whereas a symbol is connected with some abstract idea. What follows is a list of Freudian and other symbols that will be of use whatever approach you are taking to poetry.

But first a word of warning. Like biography, symbols cannot provide you with a ready-made interpretation: you have to read the symbol in the context of the whole poem and sometimes find out more about the poet to fully understand. For example, it's an easy assumption to work out that the chapel in Blake's *The Garden of Love* stands for religion and specifically Christianity. But you will also need to take into account the fact that the gates of the chapel are shut, 'thou shalt not' is written over the door and that the other religious images in the poem are lifeless and forbidding, to fully grasp the symbolic meaning of the chapel. Some poets will take a symbol off the shelf but others will invent their own and develop them in individual poems. So, use the following symbols with caution.

ACTIVITY 59

Key Skills: Communication – discussion

In a small group brainstorm possible meanings for the following symbols, bearing in mind that context may change their meaning:

- Gun
- Shadow
- Water
- Birds
- Earth
- Air
- Fruit

- Fire
- Black
- Green
- A circle
- A rose
- Flowers

TO26227

COMMENTARY   For the reasons indicated by Ted Hughes above, the following is not an 'answer' but a brief guide to the interpretation of symbols in poetry:

The phallic symbol: this is a penis or anything that represents it, and it can raise its head in an alarmingly versatile number of ways! For example: rifles, daggers, weapons of various kinds, ploughs and other tools, towers, horses and other large powerful animals, anything long and hard. It can stand for male power, sometimes in a violent or destructive sense, but also in the sense of fertility. Beware of getting too carried away here – make sure that your suggestions are supported by the wider context. These symbols can be particularly useful if you are a feminist!

The shadow: this can stand for the dark side, the primitive side of ourselves or something more sinister. It was famously used by T. S. Eliot in *The Hollow Men* (1925) where he writes:

Between the idea
And the reality
Between the motion
And the act
Falls the Shadow

The elements:
Water: this can often stand for re-birth or cleansing because of its use in baptism as a part of Christian mythology.
Air: the spirit, freedom (similar to breath and wind).
Fire: passion, life.
Earth: This could symbolise the source of life, as in the phrase 'mother earth', protection.

Birds: The Romantic poets often wrote about birds – they represent the sublime, the spirit, the soul, joy.

Colours: Some meanings will be very familiar here. For example: black symbolises negative forces, death, ignorance, disaster; red stands for life, fire, emotion, passion, strength, joy; white suggests purity, truth or, on the other hand, fear and coldness; green stands for renewal, fertility, hope. But don't forget that colours will also have personal meanings for some poets as, for example, when Hardy writes of his wife's 'air-blue gown' in an affectionate memory.

A rose: This has many symbolic meanings; for example – perfection, desire, beauty, romantic and sensual love.

Fruit: By association with the myth of the Garden of Eden, fruit is often a symbol of temptation, transgression or guilt, pleasure or desire, plenty. Apples, in particular, stand for temptation or immortality. See, for example, Blake's *A Poison Tree* or William Carlos Williams' *This Is Just to Say*.

Flowers: Beauty, innocence, youth, gentleness, the shortness of life.

A circle: This often stands for perfection, totality, unity or completeness.

ACTIVITY 60

Consider whether any of these symbols can   influence the way that you read *Valentile* (page 11).

Most of these symbols can be worked out because they are common to many cultures. Here is a myth that has become one of the most important ideas in psychoanalytic thinking:

The Oedipus myth: In the Greek plays by Sophocles, Oedipus marries his mother and murders his father. For Freud this story came to symbolise an important stage in growing up (if you are male). In other words many boys go through a phase of hating their father and feeling a strong attachment for their mother, eventually coming to identify with the father (feeling that they want to be like him) and directing amorous feelings towards girls in their peer group. If someone does not pass through this phase 'normally' then they are described as having an Oedipus complex, and in males this is usually shown through an abnormal attachment to the mother persisting into adult life. For girls, Freud mustered (with some difficulty) something called the Elektra complex – you should consult any A level psychology textbook if you are interested in pursuing this. Many critics have seen an Oedipus complex in Shakespeare's *Hamlet*, and in the context of poetry it is always worth bearing in mind in connection with poets who write about their relationship with their father or mother.

ACTIVITY 61

Some of the above symbols appear in *La Belle Dame Sans Merci* on page 65. Use them to guide an interpretation of the poem.

Psychoanalytic reading

To illustrate how psychoanalytic reading can take you into unknown and exciting territory, here is how more than one critic has applied Freud's ideas to a well-known speech in Shakespeare's *Macbeth*. The speech occurs shortly after the death of Lady Macbeth when Macbeth is reflecting upon the futility of life.

ACTIVITY 62

Some critics have found evidence in this passage that Macbeth is telling of a childhood fantasy in which he saw his mother and father having sexual intercourse. Macbeth's subsequent hatred for his father may explain his anxiety throughout much of the play. Read the following extract closely, noting any evidence that you can find for this reading. The above notes on symbols will be helpful.

Tomorrow, and tomorrow, and tomorrow,
Creeps in this petty pace from day to day,
To the last syllable of recorded time;
And all our yesterdays have lighted fools

The way to dusty death. Out, out, brief candle!
Life's but a walking shadow; a poor player,
That struts and frets his hour upon the stage,
And then is heard no more: it is a tale
Told by an idiot, full of sound and fury,
Signifying nothing.

COMMENTARY

The references to time may indicate that the fantasy has plagued Macbeth
for a long time and will continue to do so, he believes. The obvious phallic
symbol in the speech is in the reference to the candle, the rest of the speech
describing Macbeth's rejection of the fleeting pleasures ('struts and frets',
'full of sound and fury') of sex. As a result of this Macbeth has also rejected
the male role of dominance and the value of his own life ('signifying
nothing'). If you know the play you will realise that this is in keeping with
his relationship with the women in the play – all of whom dominate him.

ACTIVITY 63

Key Skills: Communication – discussion

To what extent do you agree with the above
reading? Come to your own decision and then
discuss with a partner the evidence in the
speech and in the play as a whole.

ACTIVITY 64

Below is one critic's psychoanalytic approach to
a poem by William Wordsworth. Firstly,
respond to the poem as fully as you can,
perhaps trying 'engaged reflection' as suggested
in Chapter one, and perhaps trying to predict
what kind of psychology might lie behind the
poem. Then read the critic's interpretation and
do the following:

1 In black pen, underline references to
   Wordsworth's life in the reading below.
2 In blue pen, underline ideas that you would
   consider to be psychological.
3 In red pen, underline references to the poem.
4 On the basis of the above evidence, criticise
   this reading of the poem.

A Slumber did my Spirit Seal (1800)

A slumber did my spirit seal;
I had no human fears:
She seemed a thing that could not feel
The touch of earthly years.

No motion has she now, no force;
She neither hears nor sees;
Rolled round in earth's diurnal course,
With rocks, and stones, and trees.

This poem appears in a series of poems about 'Lucy', a girl who died young. No
historical 'Lucy' has ever been found by researchers, and she appears to have been a
fiction. If we ask Freud's question of Wordsworth, 'Why did you do that?', we will
have to make up our own answer: even if he were alive, Wordsworth's own answer
could not be trusted because the real reason for the poem might well be hidden in his

unconscious. So let us ask ourselves, what wish or fear or desire might Wordsworth be expressing here in a disguised form?

When Wordsworth wrote this poem, he was living with his sister in deep poverty in Germany, enduring an extremely cold winter. His sister, Dorothy, was his lifelong companion, living with him throughout his marriage. Several of Wordworth's poems are dedicated to her; several of his poems in fact borrow from her quite brilliant journals. Wordsworth and his sister were very close.

When Wordsworth sent this poem to Samuel Coleridge, Coleridge wrote to another friend that 'in some gloomier moment' Wordsworth had 'fancied the moment in which his sister might die.' If the poem is in some way about the death of Wordsworth's sister, then it certainly does represent a profound fear for Wordsworth. And yet, the poem is oddly unemotional. The speaker 'had' no fears; 'she' feels nothing: the speaker's spirit is sleeping and sealed off ...

But why would Wordsworth refuse to acknowledge the profound grief one would expect to arise at the idea of his sister's death? A psychological view, looking at the intimacy of Wordsworth's relationship with his sister, would have to wonder if perhaps he isn't protecting himself against desires he cannot acknowledge.

Steven Lynn, Texts and Contexts

COMMENTARY There is a great deal of biography in this reading: the references to Wordsworth's relationship with his sister; Coleridge's letter. The psychological elements appear in the last paragraph in the form of Wordsworth's denial of this great fear. The poem is referred to very little but it is used to create a link between biographical facts and the psychological explanation. Perhaps the strongest criticism of this reading is that there is little reference to the poem and it is difficult to see how the psychology can take us any deeper into the poem

ACTIVITY 65

Key Skills: Communication – presentation; IT – different sources

Some critics feel that *A Slumber did my Spirit Seal* is about Margaret Hutchinson, the younger sister of Wordsworth's wife, Mary. Consult various biographical sources and return to the poem in order to choose between the two interpretations. Present your views using evidence from both the biography and the poem. Does it matter which interpretation you choose?

The activity that follows provides an opportunity to read a poem for yourself, putting right some of the shortcomings of the above example of psychological reading. Your aim is to show that, on this occasion, a psychological reading can combine elements of biography and textual analysis.

ACTIVITY 66

Key Skills: Communication – reading

Read the poem by Seamus Heaney below. It is followed by a biographical account of the poem, which is the way that it is usually approached. Use the poem and the biographical reading to create your own Freudian reading using the symbolism explained above. After responding to the poem, identify its potential symbols and proceed from there. You are advised to pursue the line of phallic symbolism and how this relates to the speaker's relationship with his father. Here are some prompts to get you started:

- Compare the way that the speaker is holding the pen compared with the way his father used the spade.
- Why does the speaker see the pen as 'squat' but also like a gun?
- If the earth is a female image, comment on the way that the father's actions with the spade are described.
- What has this poem got to do with male power?

Digging

Between my finger and thumb
The squat pen rests; snug as a gun.

Under my window, a clean rasping sound
When the spade sinks into gravelly ground:
My father, digging. I look down

Till his straining rump among the flowerbeds
Bends low, comes up twenty years away
Stooping in rhythm through potato drills
Where he was digging.

The coarse boot nestled on the lug, the shaft
Against the inside knee was levered firmly.
He rooted out tall tops, buried the bright edge deep
To scatter new potatoes that we picked
Loving their cool hardness in our hands.

By God, the old man could handle a spade.
Just like his old man.

My grandfather cut more turf in a day
Than any other man on Toner's bog.
Once I carried him milk in a bottle
Corked sloppily with paper. He straightened up
To drink it, then fell to right away

Nicking and slicing neatly, heaving sods
Over his shoulder, going down and down
For the good turf. Digging.

The cold smell of potato mould, the squelch and slap
Of soggy peat, the curt cuts of an edge
Through living roots awaken in my head.
But I've no spade to follow men like them.

Between my finger and my thumb
The squat pen rests
I'll dig with it.

from Death of a Naturalist

A Biographical reading of *Digging*

This is not a complex poem, but it has some startling features. The poem begins with Heaney writing, pen in hand. Under the window, his father digs the garden ('flowerbeds'), reminding Heaney how his father and, twenty years before that, his grandfather had dug potatoes and turf, with craftlike perfection. Turf is what in England is called 'peat'. It is used for fuel. Heaney can't handle a spade like that, but he'll dig with the pen.

Heaney then seems to be observing a break with the past. Of the three men in the poem, grandfather, father, and son, it is the son who is the odd man out: 'But I've no spade to follow men like them.' Nonetheless he asserts a continuity, in that the action of digging, which is the running image throughout the poem ('My father digging... where he was digging ...'), is identical with Heaney's own future use for his pen: 'I'll dig with it.' Poetry will be used as a means of revealing, ('buried the bright edge deep/To scatter new potatoes.') The potatoes, which his father's digging had revealed, were objects of perfection and regard, much as poems are ('Loving their cool hardness in our hands'). So too digging means going beyond the ordinary surfaces ('down and down/For the good turf'), just as poems are meant to go beyond surfaces. The 'cuts of an edge/Through living roots' awaken in Heaney's mind roots at once living and in process of severance. The memories and the traditions impel Heaney to see his own poetic vocation as one more man digging. Throughout the poem words and images are applied to digging which suggest its qualities as craft and its associated techniques: '*clean* rasping sound', Stooping in *rhythm*', 'nestled on the lug', 'levered firmly', 'bright edge', 'Nicking and slicing neatly'. There is no sense that the pen is mightier than the spade. Indeed the reverse. The sedentary habits of the poet are hinted at. Heaney is withdrawn from the action, even from the activeness of his father's old age in the garden. Instead he is inside the window, looking on. The pen is 'squat' as opposed to the almost elegant words applied to the spade and its uses. The poet is seen in memory as a child who once carried to his grandfather milk in a bottle. The bottle is 'corked sloppily' and this contrasts with the father's firmness and vigour of body ('He straightened up/ To drink it, then fell to right away/Nicking and slicing neatly'). But, at the same time, since the pen too will be used 'to dig', all the craft-qualities of digging apply to the poetic vocation. And so continuity in difference is asserted.

Ronald Tamplin, *Seamus Heaney: Open Guides to Literature*, Open University Press, 1989

> **If we can find unconscious meanings in a poem, does that mean the author's intentions are irrelevant?**

ACTIVITY 67

Go back to the poem *Thoughts drifting through the Fat Black Woman's head* ... on page 47 – is it possible to read this poem psychologically rather than through race or gender? Here are some questions to prompt you:

■ How would you describe someone who is obsessed with their own body?

■ How would you describe someone who compares themselves with the sea and the sky?

■ What kind of character is suggested by the putting down of powerful institutions?

■ What is your reaction to someone who uses the word 'steatopygous'?

Summary

This chapter has provided a basic introduction to psychological and psychoanalytic approaches to the study of poetry. Such approaches usually focus on the poem and the poet, often when the poetry is of a confessional nature. There is a digression into the language of symbols followed by some examples of psychoanalytical readings offered by critics. This approach to literature provides an interesting answer to a question that students frequently ask: could the poet really have intended everything that critics have discovered in the poems? The point with psychoanalytic explanations is that the poet could not intend the meanings because they were unconscious and therefore beyond conscious control. This neatly bypasses the problem of what the poet really meant – if you still have hang-ups in that direction!

Further Reading

Richard Appignanesi and Oscar Zarate, *Freud for Beginners*, Icon Books, 1990. An amusing approach through cartoons.

J. C. Cooper, *The Illustrated Encyclopaedia of Traditional Symbols*, Thames and Hudson Ltd, 1978.

Terry Eagleton, *Literary Theory: an Introduction*, Blackwell, 1983. A philosophical introduction for university students.

Steven Lynn, *Texts and Contexts: Writing about Literature with Critical Theory*, Harper Collins, 1994. This is an excellent book that explains theory and gives plenty of examples. See the chapter 'Minding the Work: Psychological Criticism'.

Jack Tresidder, *A Dictionary of Symbols*, Duncan Baird, 1999.

6 Living Poems into Dead Boxes? Structuralist Approaches

The rigid rule of mathematics cannot measure life, truth or beauty. But poetry can.

Valentile

We touch under glaze,
hands fused in the firing.
Two clays baked as one.

Structuralist criticism in action

The poem seems to be built around the following opposition:

The analysis is built around a binary opposition

The idea of two:
('We', 'hands', 'two' 'clays')

unity or oneness:
('one', 'fused', 'firing')

The poem describes the process of becoming united through love – of moving from the two to the one. It develops through three stages: from initial contact ('touch' – 'glaze'), to the intensity of passion ('fused') to the final state of unity ('baked'). These three stages, marked by the three lines of the poem, show the move from one side of the opposition to the other. Each line in itself also moves from the idea of 'two' (at the beginning of each line) towards this state of unity (at the end of each line).

Typically, this approach breaks a poem down into sections or units

Explains how the poem uses the oppositions

Backed up by close reference to language

Read the following letter:

Meaningless Verse

The best definition of poetry I have encountered was that of the Nobel Prize-winning theoretical physicist Paul Dirac, who hated it.

He learnt that a subordinate wrote poetry in his spare time. He summoned the young man and said: 'How can you do both physics and poetry? In physics we try to explain in simple terms something that nobody knew before. In poetry we do the exact opposite.'

The Week, 21st Oct 2000, originally in *The Times*, Dr Roe, St Albans

At the risk of stereotyping, scientists sometimes have the reputation of viewing poetry, like the writer of the above letter, as something that clouds rather than clarifies meaning. Structuralism was an attempt, beginning in the 1960s, to give analysis of literature the respectability of science. Structuralists came nearest, of all the literary theorists, to a mathematical approach to literature, so, if you are combining your study of Literature with a science, this approach may appeal to you. Some people would argue that structuralism is out-dated but it is certainly important in the history of literary theory and it has significant advantages:

- Structuralist approaches can incorporate several other approaches without contradiction. In other words you can use structuralist techniques to support, for example, a feminist reading if you wish.
- Structuralism provides precise tools for analysing texts.

There is little point in trying to carry out a 'pure' structuralist analysis. And the term itself is not worth worrying about too much. It came about when literary theorists in the 1950s began to see parallels between language and literature: just as grammar describes the rules for language, they thought it ought to be possible to discover the rules for literature. The best strategy is to take the most useful bits from structuralism and then go your own way.

Learning to drive 2: Binary oppositions at the traffic lights

One of the most useful bits of structuralism is the idea of binary oppositions. These are basically concepts that seem to divide 'naturally' into two parts. Take, for example, traffic lights. Traffic lights revolve around the opposition 'stop' versus 'go', with the orange light acting as a link between the two. Some people would argue that all human thought revolves around such oppositions, as when someone is described as intelligent; what this really means is that the person is being contrasted with someone who is not intelligent. Or when something is described as dark this only really makes sense in contrast to something that is light.

ACTIVITY 68

In a pair generate further oppositions in addition to the ones given below. Are these natural divisions or are they created by society?

Good v evil   Left v right   Individual v Social

Using oppositions

The following poem was written by John Keats in 1819. Either read and respond to the poem to get the feel of it or read it alongside the analysis that follows. Then try the activity.

La Belle Dame sans Merci: a Ballad

O what can ail thee, knight-at-arms,
Alone and palely loitering?
The *sedge* has withered from the lake,
And no birds sing.

The title means 'Beautiful Lady without Pity'

sedge – rushes

O what can ail thee, knight-at-arms,
So haggard and so woe-begone?
The squirrel's granary is full,
And the harvest's done.

I see a lily on thy brow,
With anguish moist and fever-dew,
And on thy cheeks a fading rose
Fast withereth too.

I met a lady in the meads,
Full-beautiful – a faery's child,
Her hair was long, her foot was light,
And her eyes were wild.

There is a change of point of view in the fourth stanza

I made a garland for her head,
And bracelets too, and fragrant *zone*;
She looked at me as she did love,
And made sweet moan.

zone – a girdle or belt

I set her on my pacing steed,
And nothing else saw all day long,
For sidelong would she bend, and sing
A faery's song.

She found me roots of relish sweet,
And honey wild and manna-dew,
And sure in language strange she said –
'I love thee true'.

She took me to her elfin *grot*,
And there she wept and sighed full sore,
And there I shut her wild wild eyes
With kisses four.

grot – grotto

And there she lulled me asleep
And there I dreamed – Ah woe betide! –
The latest dream I ever dreamt
On the cold hill side.

I saw pale kings and princes too,
Pale warriors, death-pale were they all;
They cried – 'La Belle Dame sans Merci
Thee hath *in thrall*!'   *in thrall* – as a slave

I saw their starved lips in the *gloam*,   *gloam* – dusk
With horrid warning gaped wide,
And I awoke and found me here,
On the cold hill's side.

And this is why I *sojourn* here   *sojourn* – wait
Alone and palely loitering,
Though the sedge is withered from the lake,
And no birds sing.

Analysis of stanzas 1–4 using binary oppositions

The following table shows an analysis in progress, with comments on the right hand side. The opposition 'life' versus 'death' suggests itself to the reader on the basis of reading the first stanza.

Life	Death
	ail
	palely loitering
	withered
	no birds sing
	ail
granary is full	harvest's done

Several words so far suggest that death is close. Will life actually appear?

The squirrel's granary suggests hoarding for winter (= death). Does it suggest resistance to death by nature?

At this point further oppositions seem to emerge: nature's 'death' seems to be accepted – the poet uses statements here, whereas the knight's 'death' is questioned, or not accepted, so we get:

human world	nature
death questioned	'death' unquestioned

Does this suggest that there is something unnatural about the knight's 'death' – connected with Keats' early death?

In stanza three there are several images of death ('fading rose', 'fever dew') but these are represented by flowers that are associated with parts of the knight's body. So the 'nature'-'human world' opposition breaks down? Perhaps they are dying because they are associated with the knight? The lily symbolises purity and the rose beauty (see *Brewer's Dictionary of Phrase and Fable*, Cassell). Does this imply that the knight would normally be in tune with nature but is not now?

lady	knight
Full-beautiful	haggard
Hair long, foot light	Cheeks – fading rose

There is a contrast in the physical descriptions of knight and lady, but where does 'wild' fit in?

'Wild' might appear as something of a surprise but it begins to raise further oppositions. The lady has the beauty that the knight once had. But whereas the knight was once 'pure', 'wild' suggests something animalistic. 'Faery's child' might suggest innocence but it also hints at something that is beyond nature. So the poet is opening up a distinction between 'beautiful' and 'pure'.

ACTIVITY 69

Continue to analyse *La Belle Dame sans Merci* using binary oppositions as shown above or using your own beginning if you disagree with the analysis so far. Use tables and diagrams as much as you can. Then use the analysis to form your own reading of the poem.

Is structuralism, as presented here, too crude and mechanical for use in responding to poetry?

Beyond oppositions

Binary oppositions were supposed to lead to nice neat analyses of poems, exposing the workings of completely enclosed systems with no thought given to the contexts surrounding the poem. For structuralists there was no need to look outside the poem to biographies or the society in which the poem was written. However, we now know that this idea was misguided and that the meanings of poems spill out into the life of the poet, into the society in which he/she lived and even into your lives, to name but three examples.

When post-structuralists came along after the 1960s they began to wonder if it was possible to pin down the meaning of a poem at all. Words always seem to imply something else, no matter how you try to nail them. Every association can trigger off a new association into infinity. Even when dealing with binary oppositions in the above section, the opposition between 'natural' and 'human' began to break down in the first stanza with the mention of 'harvest'. After all, 'harvest' is something that is dictated by the cycle of the seasons and so it is natural. But, from another point of view, it might suggest the human exploitation of natural resources. So which side of the 'natural'/'human' opposition are we to put it? When you get to a point where you think a poem is undoing or criticising itself, you are doing post-structuralism.

ACTIVITY 70

Look again at the structualist reading of *Valentile* at the beginning of this chapter. Examine closely the words that contribute to the main opposition in the poem and then try to pick them apart. You might begin by questioning the poem's central metaphors –

every metaphor breaks down at some point – for example, how adequate do you find the metaphor 'baked'? Is there any sense in which it might suggest the opposite of what was intended?

ACTIVITY 71

Continue to look for oppositions in *La Belle Dame sans Merci* until you begin to find things that contradict another part of the poem. Is it

possible to show in this way that the poem really does not make sense?

Story structures: living poems into dead boxes?

One of the more enduring aspects of structuralist theory has been story structures. These are more often applied to prose than poetry, but in the present context they offer a fresh, unusual approach. There is a tendency to break a poem down into its parts, according to given definitions, just as when the changing of traffic lights was broken down into three phases (see p84). Some critics see this approach as sterile and mechanical – just squeezing a living poem into dead boxes – but if you see it as a means towards a personal response you can bring the poem back to life again with additional insights. There is no reason why you should feel restricted by rigid categories – just use them to get you thinking more deeply.

Time and point of view

The organisation of point of view and time are two important aspects of any kind of story-telling. In traditional fairy tales no one is interested in how the wolf felt and flashbacks are sometimes necessary to show how the hero felt earlier. Structuralists interested in narrative have done a great deal of work showing how writers can manipulate time and point of view to produce certain 'effects' from their writing.

Point of view:

If there is a character in the poem, are we experiencing that character's point of view? This may be expressed through the first person ('I') or the third person ('he'/'she'). Is one character's point of view privileged over another's? In other words, are we restricted to an outside view of one of the characters? For example, in *La Belle Dame sans Merci* we experience only the lady's outwardly observable actions apart from 'she did love', which seems to have been a mistaken assumption on the part of the knight-at-arms. This raises an important issue of how reliable the narrator is – can the reader take at face value everything that he says? So the important questions are:

■ Whose point of view?
■ How many points of view?
■ An external (visual) or an internal (feelings etc.) view of characters?

In *La Belle Dame sans Merci* there are two points of view. The first may be Keats' and the second is the knight-at-arms. As feminists might point out, the lady's point of view is excluded from the poem. But we might also ask why the poem does not return to 'Keats'' point of view at the end.

ACTIVITY 72

Use the above questions on point of view to guide an analysis of a poem you are studying. Look closely at the language to see if it reflects the point of view of a 'character' in the poem. Consider too what 'external' points of view are included or excluded from the poem. For example, does it include women, powerful people, a historical perspective, the poor, or any other group you can think of? Where does the poet fit into this? You might begin by considering the points of view mentioned in *Break, Break, Break* (page 85).

ACTIVITY 73

The sonnet *In the Park* (page 35) arguably contains a subtle shift of point of view. Think about who is seeing the action and which verbs indicate this. How does the point of view reflect the poem as a whole?

Time:

The undoing of temporal (to do with time) nuts and bolts can reveal things about a poem that you might otherwise take for granted. The organisation of time is usually broken down into three related aspects:

Duration: How long is spent (in terms of number of words) on various sections of the narrative? Does the text summarise or does it try to recreate a scene? Does it describe so that no story time goes by, using mainly the verb 'to be'? In *La Belle Dame sans Merci* the use of dialogue creates a sense of immediacy, of two people standing before us talking, but the story proper does not begin until the fourth stanza with 'I met ...'. There is no sense of the duration of any event in the poem except in the words 'all day long' and this perhaps contributes to a feeling of timelessness, of suspended animation.

Frequency: The important question here is how often did something happen and how many times is it actually narrated? For example, in *La Belle Dame sans Merci* there is a repetition of the action in the first and last stanzas even though it is effectively the same event. This gives the poem a sense of completion and adds emphasis to the knight's sense of hopelessness. You could also argue that the dream is narrated three times: 'there I dreamed', 'the latest dream I ever dreamt' and in the next six lines – which create a scene from the previous summaries. Perhaps the point of this is to build the dramatic tension as the story reaches its climax.

Order: the question is – in what order are the events narrated? In *La Belle Dame sans Merci* they are largely chronological except that most of the action of the poem is a flashback to what has already happened. 'The latest dream I ever dreamt' is ominous in that it seems to suggest no more dreams in the future.

ACTIVITY 74

The following extract is taken from Milton's *Paradise Lost* (1667), probably the greatest narrative poem ever written. This epic tells the story of The Fall of Man – based on the story of the Garden of Eden and Adam and Eve's expulsion from the garden. The extract covers Satan's reactions to his own expulsion into hell for challenging the power of God, having once been one of the brightest angels. The first 'he' referred to is Beelzebub, Satan's partner who has also been expelled. Satan later also reflects on his feelings towards God's power.

Note that this material is dense and will require several readings. The suggested approach will offer only an initial way into the text rather than access to a fuller analysis. The extract has been divided into sections (using bold and normal font), each dealing with a different time zone: past, present or future. Decide which is which, using adverbials of time such as, 'now' and verb tenses to help you. Then consider the following questions:

1 How does the passage change with respect to time as it progresses?
2 What impression do you get of Satan as a result of this method of organisation?
3 Do you agree with the many critics who have argued that Satan is an attractive character?

Book 1, Lines 84–116

If thou beest he; but O how fall'n how chang'd
From him, who in the happy Realms of Light
Cloth'd with transcendent brightness didst outshine
Myriads though bright: If he whom mutual league,
United thoughts and counsels, equal hope
And hazard in the Glorious Enterprize,
Joynd with me once, **now misery hath joynd**
In equal ruin: into what Pit thou seest
From what highth fall'n, so much the stronger prov'd
He with his Thunder: and till then who knew
The force of those dire Arms? **yet not for those,**
Nor what the Potent Victor in his rage
Can else inflict, do I repent or change,
Though chang'd in outward lustre; **that fixt mind**
And high disdain, from sense of injur'd merit,
That with the mightiest rais'd me to contend,

And to the fierce contention brought along
Innumerable force to Spirits arm'd
That durst dislike his reign, and me preferring,
His utmost power with adverse power oppos'd
In dubious Battle on the Plains of Heav'n,
And shook his throne. What though the field be lost?
All is not lost; th' unconquerable Will,
And study of revenge, immortal hate,
And courage never to submit or yield:
And what is else not to be overcome?
That Glory never shall his wrath or might
Extort from me. To bow and sue for grace
With suppliant knee, and deifie his power,
Who from the terrour of this Arm so late
Doubted his Empire, that were low indeed,
That were an ignominy and shame beneath
This downfall;

Summary

This chapter has concentrated on a few limited aspects of structuralism: binary oppositions, the organisation of time and point of view. It is useful at times to consider that binary oppositions often break down.

ACTIVITY 75

Key Skills: Communication – reading

Many critics (e.g. Richard Webster) see the opposition between violence and tenderness as crucial to Ted Hughes' early poetry. Using poems that you have studied by Hughes, explore this relationship.

ACTIVITY 76

Helen Phillips writes about Chaucer's *Knight's Tale*: 'It is a tale founded on opposites. Love involves both harmony and suffering; war brings both honour and destruction. The narrative presents the world in terms of polarities, rivalries and contrasts: Thebes and Athens, Venus and Mars, man and woman, youth and maturity.' Explore how the story deals with these opposites as the tale progresses. For example, are these differences resolved or do they remain polarities, always a problem?

ACTIVITY 77

You will find oppositions at work in most poetry and these can make satisfying targets for analysis. Some examples are: the tension between continuity with the past and breaking with the past in the early work of Seamus Heaney; destruction versus joy in Yeats' poetry; the benevolence or wildness of nature in Hardy's poetry. By using a spider diagram and a large sheet of paper, identify an important opposition in the poetry you are studying and explore its significance.

Order, duration and frequency can most easily be applied to narrative poetry but they can also be fruitful with any poem that creates a scene or situation. Here are some poets whose work can be illuminated by this approach: Robert Browning, Geoffrey Chaucer, Samuel Taylor Coleridge, Lord Tennyson, Alexander Pope, Thomas Hardy. Questions to ask are: what is the effect of this order of events? What does this frequency or duration of events emphasise or hide? How could the poem have been presented otherwise and what difference would this have made?

Further Reading

Michael J. Toolan, *Narrative: A Critical Linguistic Introduction*, Routledge, 1988. A comprehensive but challenging book for students.

Voice of the Shuttle, http://vos.ucsb.edu This is a vast web site aimed at university students, with extensive sections on literary theory. For binary oppositions see 'monstrous boundaries – the embodiment of things that frighten society'.

7 Why Shouldn't She? Reading Like a Woman

Poetry is a lie which makes us realise truth.

Valentile

We touch under glaze,
hands fused in the firing.
Two clays baked as one.

Feminism in action

Gender as a theme is immediately apparent

This is the beginning of the put-down of the male perspective

The poem is about male power which confuses a love-interest with a personal interest in ceramics. It appears to be a light-hearted valentine but the poet is intent on cleverly displaying his ability to extend a metaphor ('fused') and use word-play ('valentile') all neatly wrapped up in a haiku. Any mention of the recipient of the poem (who is known to be female) has been cleverly eliminated by the use of the pronoun 'we' – notice how, with typical male egotism, the poet assumes they are together (in the 'we') even before they are 'fused': and he presumes to speak for both of them throughout, using plurals until he reaches the sinister 'one'. This word pretends a romantic union but it can only refer to the 'one' who has been dominant throughout – the poet himself. The finality of his over-confident assertions is emphasised by the monosyllabic words of the last line.

Refers to what the poem does not say as well as what it does

Reference to language

Close reference to language with example

Moves from language feature to attitude of 'speaker'

There are more jokes about feminism than any other literary perspective, as when you hear someone say: everyone knows that there are two kinds of women in the world – feminists and real women. Or: Why did the feminist cross the road? Answer: Why shouldn't she? Maybe feminism has this reputation because it has constantly sought to challenge male values and the jokes are a kind of revenge. But even female critics are aware of this negative image:

Feminism today has become a bogey, a whipping boy, routinely produced to explain all social ills: women's struggle for equality of choice in matters of sex, their grasp of sovereignty over their bodies, are blamed in particular for the rise in family breakdown, the increase in divorce, and the apparently spiralling delinquency and violence of children.

Marina Warner, *Managing Monsters*

But really all that feminists are trying to do is stand up for women and their way of seeing things. So much of our popular culture is built around the differences between men and women – you only have to watch the soaps for an evening or read the popular press. She is sensitive and he is violent; she wants to renew marriage vows and he is having an affair; she is labelled a whore but he is just a bit of a lad, and so on. Although there are clearly many similarities between the ways that men and women see the world, there are also undeniable differences, as these examples testify. So why shouldn't poetry also reflect these differences? Why shouldn't a woman read a poem differently from a man? Why shouldn't a critic be a complete sexist who needs to be put right?

It is perhaps best to treat feminist readings as a game, a kind of role that you have to play when you are studying literature. This does not mean that you have to be insincere: commitment to what you are saying is an advantage whether it is a role play or not. The rules are simple: you ask yourself how a woman would read this poem. You may be thinking that this is impossible for men and pointless for women. But this is not so. Men must simply open themselves up to their idea of a female perspective and women must remind themselves of a part of themselves (their womanhood) that the text may be trying to make them forget. Many feminists also argue that women in fact read like men because they have been indoctrinated by a male-dominated world.

One of the advantages of feminist readings is that images of men and women are common in poetry and so they provide a wealth of material for interpretation.

How might a woman read differently from a man?

ACTIVITY·79

Key Skills: Communication – discussion

Consider the kinds of experiences and attitudes that might lead women to read poetry differently from men. For example, you might like to consider: women's attitude to relationships, sex and marriage; women's sensitivity to matters of the heart; consciousness of women's historical ill-treatment and under-representation in matters of science and politics. Don't worry at this stage about thinking in stereotypes.

ACTIVITY 80

Key Skills: Communication – discussion

Using ideas like the above, discuss how the following subjects might be read or perceived differently by men and women. All of these topics have been dealt with by major poets (mainly male).

- Love
- The Fall of Man
- Childhood
- The First World War
- The death of King Arthur
- God
- Making the most of time
- The Vietnam War
- Growing old together
- Waking up in the morning with your lover

COMMENTARY

Here are a few suggestions: men might see love as a trap, woman might see it as something very valuable; The Fall of 'Man' might be reinterpreted by women as a frame-up of Eve; in recent years women's writing about childhood is perhaps more inclined to break stereotypes; women might see war as a problem arising from male aggression whereas men might emphasise the political or tragic aspects. The ways that men and women read these ideas depends very much on whether you take a traditional or a progressive view of gender. However, it is unlikely that men and women will have different views on everything just because they are men and women.

Can a man read like a woman?

Images of women in poetry

To argue any kind of feminist position you will need to have some knowledge of concepts, images and myths associated with ideas of maleness and femaleness. You will then need to apply them to the poems you are studying.

ACTIVITY 81

1 Which of the images below is favourable and which unfavourable to women?
2 In a small group, brainstorm stories, films or poems in which you have found the following images of women.

- *Enclosure:* there is a myth that women have throughout history been 'enclosed' or restricted by men. This can be taken as a metaphor for the way that women are, for example, less likely than men to become an MP or the boss of a large company. It's a way of keeping women in their place.

- *Women are traditionally associated with:* nurturing, feelings rather than intellect, beauty rather than bravery, submission rather than dominance, and so on. The list is comprised of stereotypes. Can you think of any more?

- *Green world myth:* this is the idea that women are associated with nature rather than society. Some narratives show women retreating into the green world, beyond the control of men.

- *Angels or whores?* The twentieth-century feminist Simone de Beauvoir claimed that women had either been presented in literature as spiritually perfect or as sexually promiscuous and likely to lead to the downfall of men.

- Following the above it is essential to know *the myth of the Fall of Man or the story of the Garden of Eden.* Adam and Eve live in a state of perfection but are forbidden by God to eat from the apple tree. Eve is tempted by the devil and then gets Adam to enjoy the fruits of the garden. They are both expelled from the garden and humanity has lived in a state of sin ever since. Watch out for apples as symbols!

- *Cinderella stories:* these are about potentially beautiful but badly mistreated young women who grow up to be discovered by a prince and thenceforth blossom. The Cinderella, the ugly sisters, and the prince are types to look out for.

- *The Bildungsroman:* this is usually a novel of development showing how a character grows up (for example, Jane Austen's *Emma*). This idea can be applied to longer narrative poetry. Consider, for example, Wordsworth's *The Prelude.*

- *The Mother-in-law.* Critic Elaine Millard sums up: 'Of all stereotypes none is so hated as the false, or replaced mother; in both myth and joke this figure attracts to itself all the most despised human characteristics. If to be female in a patriarchal system [dominated by males] is to be a lesser being, then femininity reaches the nadir [the lowest point] in the shape of the menopausal female ..., particularly if widowhood or celibacy places her outside direct patriarchal control ... In her mythological and historical configurations are included Lilith, the Great Whore of Babylon, Medusa, Jezebel, Duessa, the wife of Bath, a multiplicity of hags and crones, and every comedian's mother-in-law.' You will probably need to check up some of these in an encyclopaedia.

From *Literary Theory at Work*

ACTIVITY 82

Which of the above apply to Keats' *La Belle Dame sans Merci* on page 65?

ACTIVITY 83

Key Skills: Communication – reading

It's important to remember that taking a feminist approach is as much about images of men as it is about those of women. Using the above images as a starting point, investigate popular and cultural images of men. Do some research using the internet and encyclopedias so that you come up with a list similar to the above. See also the further reading at the end of the chapter. What conclusions can you draw by comparing the two lists?

What does a feminist critic say?

To read like a feminist you need to adopt the right kind of language when you write. In feminist criticism you will find phrases like those in the activity below.

ACTIVITY 84

The phrases below have been taken from the work of a feminist critic.

a Create categories of words that seem to go together because of their similarity of meaning. For example, 'bitterness' and 'hatred' can obviously be linked.

b Discuss your impressions of what feminism is trying to achieve on the basis of these findings.

Asserting female identities . . .
Re-creating women's experiences of . . .
Contemplate the fates and resistances of many women . . .
These poems articulate the bitterness . . .
She is not just a victim . . .
Other poems invoke her silent hatred . . .
. . . have a double meaning . . .
articulating anger and resistance . . .
dismantling stereotype . . .
She speaks for other women as well as herself . . .
Inverting the traditional sexual roles by making the woman active . . .
The female reader . . . comes to recognise her place as 'other' . . .
The silence of the female characters . . .
Lack of control over language . . .
Women's marginality in language and society . . .
. . . powerlessness for women . . .
The girls signify nothing . . .

COMMENTARY

Here is one possible arrangement of the key ideas in these extracts:

1 powerlessness, signify nothing, marginality, 'other', victim, lack of control
2 bitterness, hatred, anger and resistance, resistances
3 female identities, women's experiences, stereotype, traditional sexual roles, fates
4 silence, silent, articulating, articulate, speaks, language, language and society
5 inverting, dismantling, asserting, active
6 re-creating, invoke, to recognise, contemplate.

Can you justify any other arrangement? Has anything been missed out of this list?

ACTIVITY 85

In a pair, explain why you think the above ideas have been arranged in these groups. If it helps, give each list a title.

ACTIVITY 86

In the above extracts what kinds of issues are feminist critics concerned with? Are there any extracts which you think are not explicitly feminist? If you had to produce a list of dimensions on which feminists view literature, what would they be (some critics call these oppositions)? Complete a chart like the following, adding your own dimensions:

Powerful --------------------------------- powerless

COMMENTARY

Feminist critics are concerned with issues such as who has power and who has not, or who is seen to be the more powerful – males or females. 'Asserting identities' means trying to show women as they really are, sometimes by retelling a story from the point of view of women and capturing the experience of women that has not been told. This dimension might be called 'identity – anonymity'. Here are some other dimensions used by feminists:

- Perpetrator – victim
- Resistance – acceptance
- Stereotype – reality?
- Speaking out – silence
- Active – passive

You may have noticed that these are also examples of binary oppositions. These are covered in more detail on page 64.

ACTIVITY 87

Key Skills: Communication – reading

Do a survey of any set of poems you are studying by applying the above dimensions. Count the number of references to women in the poems and then categorise them according to the above dimensions. What conclusions can you draw from this exercise? Alternatively, you could check out the 'political correctness' of this book by surveying the poems included in each chapter.

Going with the flow: who does the poem want you to be?

Tin-openers and saucepans usually expect you to be right-handed, although, interestingly, washing machine doors assume that you are using your left. Left-handed people will know how awkward these things can be.

For some feminists problems with interpretation start because the poem assumes a male reader and the attitudes that go with him. Every poem you read, every text you read, suggests the reader that it wants. But how can they do this?

An obvious starting point for the argument is newspaper headlines. If you want some quick proof that texts imply different kinds of readers, buy a few newspapers on the same day with headlines about the same topic. When you see a *Sun* headline that reads 'Rat Doped His Bride and Went Next Door for Nookie' there are certain things implied about the readers: first that they would be interested in such titillating material and, second, that they would go along with the lack of seriousness that the language, especially 'nookie', implies.

ACTIVITY 88

The following headlines appeared on the same day in various British newspapers. The story covered a change of kit by American tennis player Venus Williams. In a small group discuss the ways in which these headlines define their readers. What attitudes, interests and knowledge do they assume? To what extent do they assume male readers? Who, in other words, do they want their readers to be? The names of the newspapers that the headlines appeared in are given at the end of the chapter.

1 **When it comes to fashion, Venus is out of this world**

2 **The Venus eye trap**
3 **Fashion statement catches Williams on re-bound**
4 **Venus Williams leads off-beat fashion show**
5 **Hingis grins and Venus bares it**
6 **Venus keeps sponsors out in front**

The same idea can be applied to poetry only poetry defines readers with more subtlety. For feminists, the danger is to assume that all readers are men.

Resisting men

In order to carry out a feminist reading successfully you will need to have some idea of how to resist the conventional male reader that the text is trying to make of you. There are roughly three kinds of arguments that feminists target:

- How are women presented in the text in terms of what they do or do not do?
- What kind of language is used to present these women?
- How does the gender of the author and their views reflect the text?

The first two of these will be explored in the following section.

> **Is the 'best' reader of a poem the one who is most like the author?**

The sexiest poem in English? (if you are a man)

For many people John Donne's poem *The Sun Rising* (circa 1603) is a rampant celebration of sex. But women may find it offensive in a number of respects.

ACTIVITY 89

Key Skills: Communication – reading

a Use some of the terms explored in the last section to carry out a resistant feminist reading of this poem. Hints:

- Look at references to males and females
- Who is active and who passive?
- Look at images of power

The Sun Rising

Busy old fool, unruly sun,
　　Why dost thou thus
Through windows and through curtains call on us?
Must to thy motions lovers' seasons run?
　　Saucy *pedantic* wretch, go chide   *pedantic* – fussy
　　Late schoolboys and sour *prentices*;   *prentices* – apprentices
Go tell court huntsmen that the king will ride;
　　Call country ants to harvest offices:
Love, all alike, no season knows, nor clime,
Nor hours, days, months, which are the rags of time.

Thy beams, so *reverend* and strong   *reverend* – respected
　　Why should'st thou think?
I could eclipse and cloud them with a wink,
But that I would not lose her sight so long:
　　If her eyes have not blinded thine,
　　Look, at tomorrow late tell me
Whether both *th' Indias of spice and mine*   *th' Indias of spice and*
　　Be where thou leftst them, or lie here with me.   *mine* – the east Indies
Ask for those kings whom thou sawst yesterday,   brought spices, the west
And thou shalt hear, all here in one bed lay.   Indies gold to Europe

　　She's all states, and all princes, I;
　　Nothing else is.
Princes do but play us; compared to this,
All honour's mimic; all wealth alchemy.   *all honour's mimic; all*
　　Thou, sun, art half as happy as we,   *wealth alchemie* – their
　　In that the world's contracted thus;   love is the only worthy
Thine age asks ease, and since thy duties be   thing
　　To warm the world, that's done in warming us.
Shine here to us, and thou art everywhere:
This bed thy centre is, these walls, thy sphere.

b Using a short selection of some poems you are studying, make notes towards a feminist reading using the techniques described above.

c Find some feminist criticism for yourself and identify the kinds of phrases it uses and issues it deals with. Some recent study guides contain sections on this.

COMMENTARY In reading this poem as a feminist you might refer to the following: the apparent arrogance of the speaker (who is assumed to be male); the male-dominated world portrayed; the emphasis on the woman's physical appearance; references to male power ('the king', 'princes'); use of the colonial conquest metaphor ('she's all states', and 'both the India's'). Perhaps most blatantly there is the woman's silence and passivity.

ACTIVITY 90

Key Skills: several key skills could be developed from the following activities

Carol Ann Duffy has said of herself: 'I don't mind being called a feminist poet, but I wouldn't mind if I wasn't. I think the concerns of art can go beyond that ... I have never in my life sat down and thought 'I will write a feminist poem''. (Interview with Andrew McAllister, *Bete Noire*, 6, 1988.) Do you think that Duffy is a feminist poet, based on your reading of her poetry?

ACTIVITY 91

In *The Canterbury Tales* is Griselda in *The Clerk's Tale* the perfect wife, or is she a symbol of incomprehensible femininity that terrifies men through their inability to understand it?'

ACTIVITY 92

Return to *La Belle Dame sans Merci* on page 65. Is it possible to ignore the apparent sexism in this poem? Carry out a feminist reading of this poem using the ideas in this chapter. Instead of simply dismissing the poem because it is sexist, explore how the knight might be to blame for what happens.

ACTIVITY 93

Read the following extract by D. H. Lawrence (1885–1930) about women, written in 1930. Re-read his poem *After the Opera* on page 46 and attempt a feminist criticism. Read the poem and the extract against each other. Do you find the two pieces consistent?

The real trouble about women is that they must always go on trying to adapt themselves to men's theories of women, as they always have done. When a woman is thoroughly herself, she is being what her type of man wants her to be. When a woman is hysterical it's because she doesn't quite know what to be, which pattern to follow, which man's picture of woman to live up to...

Now the real tragedy is not that women ask and must ask for a pattern of womanhood. The tragedy is not, even, that men give them such abominable patterns, child-wives, little-boy-baby-face girls, perfect secretaries, noble spouses, self-sacrificing mothers, pure women who bring forth children in virgin coldness, prostitutes who just make themselves low, to please men; all atrocious patterns of womanhood that men have supplied to woman; patterns all perverted from any real natural fulness of a human being. Man is willing to accept woman as an equal, as a man in skirts, as an angel, a devil, a baby-face, a machine, an instrument, a bosom, a womb, a pair of legs, a servant, an encyclopedia, an ideal, or an obscenity; the one thing he won't accept her as, is a human being, a real human being of the feminine sex.

Selected Essays

Summary

This chapter has emphasised two aspects of feminism: the ways in which women might read differently from men, and the images of men and women in literature. The importance of adopting the appropriate language and concepts is also covered. Feminism is seen as a form of resistant reading – it resists the assumption that all readers are men.

Answers to activity 88, page 75. The newspapers responsible for the headlines are as follows:

1 *Daily Express*
2 *Daily Mail*
3 *The Times*
4 *Independent*
5 *Guardian*
6 *Daily Telegraph.*

Further Reading

Jan Montefiore, *Feminism and Poetry: Language, Experience, Identity in Women's Writing*, Pandora, 2000.

Brian Moon, *Studying Literature: Theory and Practice for Senior Students*, Chalkface Press, 1990. Contains a useful practical chapter on reading in terms of gender.

Marina Warner, *Six Myths of Our Time – Managing Monsters*, Vintage, 1994. This is an excellent readable book for exploring myths and the way that they are interpreted in the modern world, especially in chapters one and two.

8 Readings in Competition

Poetry, not prose, lies at the core.

Valentile

We touch under glaze,
hands fused in the firing.
Two clays baked as one.

Here are Jeremy Hughes' comments on his own poem *Valentile:*

The poem was written for my wife and given to her as a St Valentine's Day gift. She is interested in ceramic tiles and has a few displayed in our home. I wanted to give her the poetic equivalent, which expressed my love for her, and to create something that felt crafted. I also wanted to write in a particular form and considered the sonnet and the haiku. I was pressed for time, so the haiku won.

There is a problem here, though. Strictly speaking, a haiku consists of three lines of five syllables, seven syllables and five syllables. The second line of *Valentile* might have six syllables or seven syllables depending on whether you say 'firing' with two syllables or three. Purists might believe that it is only six syllables but these days haikus seem to be acceptable if they are *in the spirit of* haiku.

Because I was *writing* a tile, so to speak, the poem relies on metaphor. I also wanted the poem to be erotic, if possible, and to join us in some way. From my point of view, I like the way it moves from the verb 'touch', which is gentle and tentative like a first meeting, through the heat connotations of 'fused' to the solidifying permanence of 'baked'. The 'clays' are our bodies, of course, and the metaphysical poets and the poem 'The force that through the green fuse' by Dylan Thomas were in the back of my mind.

When I actually gave the poem to my wife, I drew the tile on mounting board as I imagined it might look, and hand wrote the poem beneath it.
(personal communication to the author)

ACTIVITY 94

Key Skills: Communication – discussion

1 Annotate this reading of *Valentile* as in the boxes at the beginnings of each chapter of this book.
2 Discuss how this reading compares with the others you read in Chapter 1. Which of the perspectives covered in this book does Hughes refer to? Does it influence the way that you now see the other readings? Do you regard an author's view as the definitive one?

The purposes of this chapter are:

■ to provide further practice at making use of the critics, especially in an A2 context
■ to help with the comparison of different interpretations
■ to provide advice about responding to examination questions
■ to show how to make use of critics without being weighed down by them.

Learning to drive 3: take another look at the lights

In Chapter 6 the contrast between 'stop' and 'go' was used to explain binary oppositions (contrasting ideas in a text). You may have noticed that although stopping and going are indeed important in dealing with traffic lights, there are in fact three colours and not two to be negotiated. In other words you were looking at an alternative interpretation to the one offered by the binary oppositions. Your interpretation may have been based around the three main ideas in 'traffic lights': 'stopping', 'getting ready' and 'going', and, of course, these things are encountered in a particular order by drivers. So, from the point of view of drivers, it could be argued that traffic lights are about three related ideas that trigger off different emotions, such as 'impatience', 'a release of tension' and 'eager anticipation' (you can work out which is which).

How can we compare these two views? One thing is certain – it is not a matter of one reading being 'right' and the other 'wrong' but you do need to have a means of judging them from your own point of view. We might begin by saying that using the opposition 'stop' and 'go' gets down to basics, the root of the whole point of traffic lights. You might also argue that the opposition holds true for everyone because society has agreed on those meanings, whereas individual responses to the different colours will depend on each individual – and on how quickly they want to get from A to B in their car! If you are a driver, the driver's personal response to the changing of the lights might have particular significance for you, especially if you have found yourself at the mercy of a hidden camera for going through an orange light. You might also argue that, as most people today are drivers, this interpretation strikes a chord with a dominant feature of our car-dominated culture. Further exploration is also easily prompted by this approach: how do drivers (or indeed pedestrians) perceive orange – as a lesser form of 'stop' or as closer to 'go'?

This analogy prepares you for comparing readings of poems.

Student dragged down by weight of criticism!

The most challenging aspect of AS and A level English literature is finding out what you believe – developing an independent voice – whilst at the same time making use of critics and various kinds of contextual information. It's a bit like the Greek myth of *Icarus*. Icarus was warned not to fly too close to the sun in case it melted his wax wings and not to fly too low in case he was sucked into the sea. Similarly, if all you do is borrow ideas from the critics and churn them out you are likely to be dragged down by the weight of second-hand views. On the other hand, if you develop a strong and independent set of opinions (reaching for the stars) that bear no relation to anything else you are likely to get too close to the sun. The trick is to fly somewhere in between, striking a balance between independence and dependence.

Resist the critics 1: expose them!

The problem with many critics is that they will make you believe everything they say! In order to challenge critics successfully you have to be aware of some of the techniques they use to beat you into submission.

- Many critics write as if what they are saying is fact rather than opinion.
- They tell us how every reader should react.
- They use persuasive techniques to convince us.

The following passage is R. H. Hutton's comment on Tennyson's *Break, Break, Break* (see page 5). It illustrates nicely how the critics can leave you gasping in agreement at their perceptiveness and turn of phrase. In other words, critics are persuasive as well as informative.

ACTIVITY 95

For this activity it will help if you have read and carried out the activity on *Break, Break, Break* on page 5. Make a copy of the passage below and underline features of the critic's writing that encourage you to agree with what he is saying. For example, the word 'observe' at the beginning could be taken as a directive giving you no choice if you are to continue reading.

Observe how the wash of the sea on the cold gray stones is used to prepare the mind for the feeling of helplessness with which the deeper emotions break against the hard and rigid element of human speech; how the picture is then widened out till you see the bay with children laughing on its shore, and the sailor-boy singing on its surface, and the stately ships passing on in the offing to their unseen haven, all with the view of helping us to feel the contrast between the satisfied and the unsatisfied yearnings of the human heart. Tennyson, like every true poet, has the strongest feeling of the spiritual and almost mystic character of the association attaching to the distant sail which takes the ship on its lonely journey to an invisible port, and has more than once used it to lift the mind into the attitude of hope or trust. But then the song returns again to the helpless breaking of the sea at the foot of the crags it cannot climb, not this time to express the inadequacy of human speech to express human yearnings, but the defeat of those human yearnings themselves. Thus does Lord Tennyson turn an ordinary seashore landscape into a means of finding a voice indescribably sweet for the dumb spirit of human loss.

ed. John Jump. From *Tennyson: The Critical Heritage*

COMMENTARY After his instruction to observe, the critic produces a long list of items ending with 'all with the view of'. The list itself is a persuasive technique but some of the items in the list are also little more than paraphrases of what is happening in the poem so we are unlikely to disagree with them. Notice that the critic then uses the pronoun 'us' in 'helping us to feel the contrast' which again invites 'us' to join him and his opinions. The critic is able to identify a 'true poet' so we ought to listen to what he has to say about this one. He then subtly slips in the word 'helpless' in front of 'breaking', which has the effect of giving the waves the human quality he wants them to have when he compares them with the defeat of human yearning in the next line. When explanation becomes difficult for critics they often themselves turn to metaphor, so that here 'Tennyson turns an ordinary seashore landscape into a means of finding a voice . . . for the dumb spirit of human loss'. As readers of literature know, metaphor is highly persuasive. One source of consolation against all of this may be that you can use the same techniques as the critics yourself!

Critical weaponry

Here is a list of things that critics do in their writing and that you should do in yours:

- quote from the poem
- refer to linguistic and poetic techniques used by the poet
- paraphrase the poet's ideas or themes
- refer to the poet's selection of a particular word rather than another
- refer to other poems by the same poet
- refer to what other critics said
- dismiss or support alternative points of view
- provide evidence from the poem or other written sources
- refer to the culture in which the poem was written
- refer to the cultures in which the poem has been read
- use persuasive techniques
- convert the poem's ideas into a more comfortable metaphor
- refer to what the poem does not say.

ACTIVITY 96

Write your own critical response to *Valentile* (or any other poem in this book) using as many of the above features as you can.

ACTIVITY 97

Key Skills: Communication – reading; IT – different sources

1 One way of avoiding being weighed down by critics' powerful persuasion is to reduce their arguments to their bare bones and then compare them with yours. If you have already responded to *Break, Break, Break*, list the points made by Hutton above and compare them with your own. Then refer back to the text to settle any disagreements.

This method is also demonstrated in Activity 98.

2 Try to expose the work of any of the critics presented in this book using the ideas explored in the last two activities.

3 Find an extract by a critic about a text that you are studying. As in the example above, analyse those elements of the extract that make it difficult to disagree with.

Why is it better to reflect for yourself before reading the critics rather than the other way round?

Resist the critics 2: use them against each other

Some examining boards will ask you to compare the views of two or more critics at A2 level.

ACTIVITY 98

Key Skills: Communication – reading

Read and respond to the following poem by Phillip Larkin. Write down about six key ideas that you feel emerge from the poem. Then read the two critics' views that follow it.

1 Write down what you consider to be the key abstract ideas in each extract.

2 What evidence is given by each critic?

3 Which of the approaches covered in this book are referred to?

4 Using the commentary that follows, say which reading you prefer and why, giving evidence from the poem.

To the Sea

To step over the low wall that divides
Road from concrete walk above the shore
Brings sharply back something known long before –
The miniature gaiety of seasides.
Everything crowds under the low horizon:
Steep beach, blue water, towels, red bathing caps,
The small hushed waves' repeated fresh collapse
Up the warm yellow sand, and further off
A white steamer stuck in the afternoon –

Still going on, all of it, still going on!
To lie, eat, sleep in hearing of the surf
(Ears to transistors, that sound tame enough
Under the sky), or gently up and down
Lead the uncertain children, frilled in white

And grasping at enormous air, or wheel
The rigid old along for them to feel
A final summer, plainly still occurs
As half an annual pleasure, half a rite.

As when, happy at being on my own,
I searched the sand for Famous Cricketers,
Or, farther back, my parents, listeners
To the same seaside quack, first became known.
Strange to it now, I watch the cloudless scene:
The same clear water over smoothed pebbles,
The distant bathers' weak protesting trebles
Down at its edge, and then the cheap cigars,
The chocolate-papers, tea-leaves, and, between

The rocks, the rusting soup tins, till the first
Few families start the trek back to the cars.
The white steamer has gone. Like breathed-on glass
The sunlight has turned milky. If the worst
Of flawless weather is our falling short,
It may be that through habit these do best,
Coming to water clumsily undressed
Yearly; teaching their children by a sort
Of clowning; helping the old, too, as they ought.

Reading 1

To the Sea (from *High Windows*) is another poem which observes the English at leisure. The poet watches families on their annual seaside holiday and recalls the family holidays of his own childhood. The scene is rendered with Larkin's customary exactness: the faint sound of transistor radios, a distant ship on the horizon, cigars and chocolate-papers littering the beach. As an adult the poet feels alienated from the activity around him ('Strange to it now ...') but he derives comfort and reassurance from the knowledge that the English seaside holiday is a tradition ('half an annual pleasure, half a rite') that 'Is still going on'. It fosters a simple, undemonstrative consideration for others: nervous children are helped to overcome their fear of the sea and the old in their wheelchairs are given the opportunity to enjoy a 'final summer'.

Alan Gardiner

Reading 2

Clearly there is some *ambivalence* in Larkin's recollection of his childhood, or in his mature attitude to it. It is *formally dismissed* as a blacked-out, unremembered time, and as such it obeys the consistent *ordinance* of Larkin's world whereby time remorselessly passes without being significantly used. That is to say, early life is caused to conform to the pessimistic pattern which Larkin, courageously deceptionless, discovers in the whole of existence. Offset against this formal blankness is a quite different attitude towards childhood and youthfulness, one of affection, and loss, and pained envy of those who briefly enjoy it now.

Peter Hollindale

ambivalence – indecision, mixed feelings;
formally dismissed – in other pieces of writing Larkin has rejected ...;
ordinance – rule

COMMENTARY

	Reading 1	Reading 2
Key abstract ideas	The English at leisure exactness alienation comfort and re-assurance undemonstrative consideration	ambivalence pessimistic pattern formal blankness affection loss pained envy
Evidence	quotation from poem	other sources ('formally dismissed')
Critical approaches	biography psychology?	psychology

ACTIVITY 99

Carry out a full analysis of *To the Sea* using your own ideas and incorporating the ideas of the two critics above.

ACTIVITY 100

Find two short passages of criticism about a poem that you are studying. Compare the two pieces of criticism using the method outlined above and draw your own conclusions about the poem.

ACTIVITY 101

Using the information about *The Miller's Tale* and *The Knight's Tale* in Chapter 3, compare the two readings below. Explain how each reading refers to fabliaux and romance but comes to a different conclusion. Use a table based on the one in the above commentary and explain which reading you find the most convincing.

Reading 1

The Miller's Tale is preceded by *The Knight's Tale*, an elaborate story of epic proportions and courtly love. Its high theme is matched by its serious diction. To follow it up with a low-life *fabliau* about ordinary, primarily sexual love offers a perfect contrast in the dramatic frame that loosely binds the *Tales*. But it does not fully account for the playing with genre . . .

There, Chaucer allows the abstract and spiritual notion of courtly love to be contaminated by the physical, by sex and bodily functions. In this way he is able to suggest that the ideal – represented in *The Knight's Tale* – is hopelessly distanced from everyday reality, that it is potentially outmoded and certainly unrealistic. Interestingly, Nicholas is the successful lover, one who blends courtly love language and physical action. His elegant speech is a charade designed to achieve his aim of 'deerne' love; it is a ploy to get Alison into bed. Thus Chaucer stretches this genre to its limits to produce a humorous tale that, nevertheless, questions the very purity of the courtly ideal invoked in the previous story in the collection.

Gail Ashton, *Studying Chaucer*
Studymates

deerne – hidden or secret

Reading 2

Traditional cultural values are deeply instilled, and the cleverness that has won Nicholas his prize is revealed as untrustworthy. Indeed, it is presented by Chaucer in *The Miller's Tale* as ultimately inadequate for sustained success. Because the cleverness is utilised for personal, selfish gratification rather than social, philanthropic purposes, it proves undesirable as a basis for social organisation... It is the very honesty of the fabliau protagonist's selfishness that makes his modes of operation unattractive as social or political foundations. Nicholas makes his own success, but he comes unstuck. In his exuberant relish of his own triumph he forgets to be intellectually vigilant and is caught out by his wimpish counterpart, Absalon.

In this way, Chaucer adds a new dimension to the fabliau. The intellectual alternative to moral constraint and decorum is shown to be as unsatisfactory as the structure it seeks to replace. *The Miller's Tale* therefore '*quites*' itself as well as *The Knight's Tale*, and by doing so it invites us to re-examine *The Knight's Tale* in the light of what *The Miller's Tale* has revealed. Chaucer has invented, with his deployment of the 'new' genre of the fabliau and his exploitation of its antagonistic relationship with the romance, a literary game in which he points up the shortcomings of literary and, by analogy, social constructs.

Caroline Cole, *Literary Review*, Vol 11, No 1, Sept 2000

quites – pays back, gets back at;
philanthropic – loving mankind, benevolent

ACTIVITY 102

A feminist reading of Chaucer's fabliaux

What makes the following text a feminist reading? Analyse its essential features using the points made in Activity 84 on page 77. If you are studying either of these tales, try to answer this criticism using any of the perspectives covered in this book.

In the fabliaux, like Chaucer's *Miller's Tale* or *Merchant's Tale*, the sexy young wives escape all moral retribution. Implicit is the assumption that a young wife is powerless to resist the advances of a fiery suitor and that doing with him what comes naturally constitutes no departure from universal feminine nature. The emphasis is on the foolishness of the old husband and the ingenuity of the wife and her lover – not on the wife's personality or moral nature as an actual person. The inability of the 'masculine' to control the 'feminine' and to live with it in a proper 'marriage' is the allegorical theme of most of ribald and antifeminist narratives.

Scholes and Kellogg, *The Nature of Narrative*, Oxford

ACTIVITY 103

Telling a different story

Key Skills: Communication – reading

Below is another reading of Seamus Heaney's *Digging* (see page 60).

1 In terms of the chapters in this book, what kind of reading is this?

2 Compare this reading with the biographical reading on page 61. Which reading do you prefer of the two? Why?

The critic Blake Morrison has just been discussing Heaney's poem *Follower* which again touches on the idea of one generation following on from the previous one:

The dilemma of following is not fully resolved in *Digging*, either, but comes closer to being. This is the best-known and most widely anthologised of all Heaney's poems, though he himself has called it 'a big coarse-grained navvy of a poem', and has conceded that 'a couple of lines in it ... have more of the theatricality of the gunslinger than the self-absorption of the digger'. There is indeed something clumpingly deliberate about the way Heaney claims kinship with his father by turning his writing implement into a violent weapon: 'Between my finger and my thumb/The squat pen rests; snug as a gun'. It is too macho, melodramatically so, and not even the insertion of the adjectives 'squat' and 'snug' can allay the feeling that the analogy is in any case not right – inaccurate visually and misleading in its implication that what follows in *Death of a Naturalist* is the work of a poetic hard man. The real interest of the image is that it seems to be over-compensating for the poet's shame at departing from lineage. The Heaneys had been associated with County Derry since Gaelic times, and the poet is only too aware of the fathers standing behind his father: 'By God, the old man could handle a spade./Just like his old man'. Heaney has spoken of the gibes he used to hear as a boy – 'the pen's lighter than the spade', 'learning's easy carried', 'Boys but this Seamus fellow is a great scholar. What book are you in now son?' – and he seeks to answer them here by presenting his poetry as a form of agriculture. His own digging implement is voluble, not 'curt' like his father's, but it performs many of the same functions, passing on tradition, extracting 'new' produce (poems, not potatoes) out of old furrows, and enjoying an intimacy with the earth. Heaney's assertion at the end – 'I'll dig with it' – has not quite the conviction he intends, but it is the best case he can mount in his first two books.

Blake Morrison, Seamus Heaney

ACTIVITY 104

Alternatives to John Donne

Respond to the reading of Donne that follows, considering the following questions:

a What is the main focus of the extract?

b What kind of evidence would you need to argue against it?

c How would attempt to improve it?

The critic who has made the most intriguing comments in this line [psychoanalytic] is John Carey, in his *Life, Mind, and Art* (Faber, 1981) ... Carey notes the sexual bravado of such poems as *Elegy: To his Mistress Going to Bed*, and wonders how far this defiant assertion of his masculinity may have been prompted by Donne's memory of witnessing the torture and execution of Catholic priests, which included their public emasculation. He also comments on the difficulties Donne must have faced in choosing to reject the Catholicism for which so many members of his family had suffered death or exile, and suggests that the preoccupation with change and infidelity, which marks many of the *Songs and Sonets*, may be understood as the displacement of Donne's guilt at what some of his friends and family must have considered his act of betrayal.

Phillip Mallett , John Donne, Selected Poems

Below are the essentials of a political/historical reading of *The Sun Rising* (page 80). To what extent was Donne expressing the political views of his age? Use these facts to challenge the feminist reading that appears on page 81.

- The reference to the king riding in the first stanza is probably to James I who came to the throne in 1602. James was known as a keen hunter.
- The Jacobean period was a time when trade in England was expanding further afield with the import of, for example, pepper and dyes.
- Donne became a mercenary and sailed with Raleigh.
- Some critics believe that Donne was the first poet to introduce colonial metaphors for the human body.
- This was a time of great uncertainty with ideas, for example the Earth being the centre of the universe, being challenged by astronomers like Copernicus.

With the critics in the exam

One of the main ways in which examination questions will test your response to 'different interpretations' is by giving you a quotation from a critic and then asking you to weigh it up against your own reading of the poem(s). This type of question breaks down into three sub-types:

1 **Where you are actually given a critic's view**: 'Emily Dickinson uses phrases that strike and penetrate like bullets.' (Robert N. Linscott) Selecting at least three poems from this collection, explore the ways in which you think that Emily Dickinson is particularly effective in her use of language and form. (AQA B, Specimen Units)

2 **Where you are not given a specific view**: Do you think that Shakespeare is optimistic or pessimistic in the Sonnets you have studied? Support your response by close reference to the ways in which Shakespeare conveys meanings by his uses of form, structure and language. (AQA B)

   Or, even less directive with respect to different interpretations: How important is the wedding guest to what you consider to be Coleridge's purposes in *The Ancient Mariner*? (AQA B)

3 **Where the poet's work has been categorised in some way**: Show how in his pair of poems *The Echoing Green* and *London*, Blake demonstrates his own thoughts and feelings about changes taking place in contemporary life. (AQA A)

   Or: What arguments, supported by evidence from his poetry, would you put forward to show that Keats was a Romantic poet? (AQA A)

> **It is crucial to realise that with types two and three you are still being assessed on your ability to evaluate and use critical positions, even though the question may not have given you them or have told you to bring them into your argument. This is why it is important to be familiar with the types of reading explored in this book.**

ACTIVITY 106

Copy out question 1, on page 92 and highlight
what you take to be the key words and phrases.

COMMENTARY

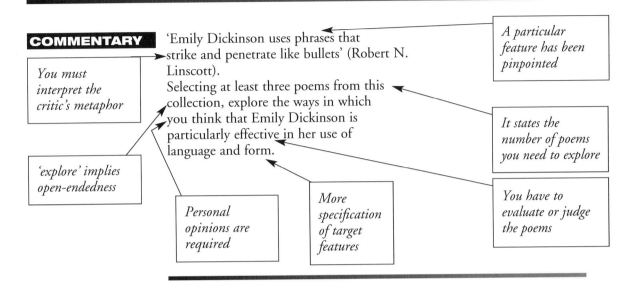

You must interpret the critic's metaphor

'explore' implies open-endedness

'Emily Dickinson uses phrases that strike and penetrate like bullets' (Robert N. Linscott).
Selecting at least three poems from this collection, explore the ways in which you think that Emily Dickinson is particularly effective in her use of language and form.

A particular feature has been pinpointed

It states the number of poems you need to explore

You have to evaluate or judge the poems

Personal opinions are required

More specification of target features

ACTIVITY 107

Attempt an answer to the question on page 92,
using Dickinson's poem on page 54.

ACTIVITY 108

Using the above analysis as a model, analyse
four more questions from your examining
board.

ACTIVITY 109

Key Skills: Communication – presentation

A worked exam question

Question: Respond to the statement 'the importance of many of Tennyson's poems lies in the settings rather than in the characters.' Choose two or three poems from the selection you have read to illustrate your answer. In your answer you should consider the following aspects: imagery, verse and style; characterisation; relationship to Tennyson's concerns and interests and his poetry as a whole. (OCR, Specimen Units)

Read the following answer to the question carefully. You do not need to know Tennyson's poetry but you may be able to take the activity further if you do. Write notes on the student's exam technique and the extent to which she is answering the question. Write the advice you would give if you were the teacher and, if possible, turn this into a presentation. If you know the poems, how would you seek to improve on this answer? Here are some initial hints for the first part of this activity:

■ Do you feel that the student has planned the answer?

- Where does she most successfully answer the question?
- Does she avoid repetition?
- How does the argument develop?

- Does she make the most of the points she raises?
- Is the vocabulary and style appropriate?

Student's answer:

I would say that the characters and what happens to them is of great importance to Tennyson and that he reflects this aspect in many of his poems. A lot of the characters suffer rather morbid experiences. Tennyson uses language, setting and scenery to enhance this factor.

Three of the poems where Tennyson's poetry is about the characters and their suffering are *Mariana*, *The Lady of Shalott*, and *Morte D'Arthur*. In *Mariana*, she is suffering through the waiting for an appearance of someone who does not materialise. The language and setting reflects her mood of wretchedness, desolation, torture:

> With blackest moss the flower-pots
> Were thickly crusted, one and all:
> The rusted nails fell from the knots
> That held the pear to the gable-wall.

Here, he is describing a scene of wrack and ruin, clearly. In the same way Mariana is decaying inside herself. Rotting away to nothing because of her loss. The characters do play an important role obviously because they are the main focus throughout the poem. It is through the setting that we can get a real feel for the poem, the characters. It helps to understand the character and the development of them better.

However, I think that the statement 'the importance of many of Tennyson's poems lies in the settings rather than in the characters,' is true to a great extent. There is a lot of mention about the setting. Again, from *Mariana*:

> And ever when the moon was low,
> And the shrill winds were up and away
> In the white curtain, to and fro
> She saw the gusty shadow sway.

and it is the setting that gives us a deeper insight into the characters. I do not feel that there are direct references to the characters themselves. Tennyson describes what Mariana is doing:

> Her tears fell with the dews at even
> Her tears fell ere the dews were dried;
> She could not look on the sweet heaven
> Either at morn or eventide.

This is describing what the character is doing and, of course, this allows us to see the mood of the character and their feelings. I think that the setting enhances things about the character:

> All day within the dreamy house
> The doors upon their hinges creak'd;
> The blue fly sung in the pane; the mouse
> Behind the mouldering wainscot shriek'd,
> Or from the crevice peer'd about.
> Old faces glimmer'd thro' the doors
> Old footsteps trod the upper floors,
> Old voices called her from without.

This allows us to build up a picture of what is going on. Some of the scenery helps with the characters too.

In *The Lady of Shallott* Tennyson writes about the character, giving a sense of confinement, that the lady is trapped:

> Four gray walls and four gray towers,
> Overlook a space of flowers,
> And the silent isle imbowers
> The Lady of Shallott.

The thought of the lady being trapped is helped by the imagery of the 'isle' engulfing her and not allowing her to escape.

In *Morte D'Arthur* there is a moroseness that runs through the poem:

> His own thought drove him like a goad.
> Dry clash'd his harness in the icy caves
> And barren chasms, and all to left and right
> The bare black cliff clang'd round him . . .

This description emphasises his thought. So I do not think that the setting necessarily carries more importance than the characters, but that it helps to enhance, understand the characters more.

COMMENTARY

Teacher's comment:

1 You have not tackled the third bullet point at all.
2 Your answer leads the reader to believe, at first, that you do <u>not</u> agree with the statement in the question. Then, later, you seem to be agreeing. It would be better to make it clear <u>at the start</u> exactly what stance you are taking.
3 *Mariana* – good, on the whole, but you tend towards repetition of general comments (which <u>are</u> accurate) rather than <u>specific</u> points, backed up by examples, to record your views.
4 *The Lady of Shalott* – what you say is relevant but it is too superficial and too brief. *Morte D'Arthur* – having chosen this poem as an example, you *must* discuss it. A time management problem?
5 Potentially, you write well about the poems but there are several areas we need to work on (there <u>is</u> time!):

■ Use of technical terms (none to speak of here).
■ Use of apt quotation – integrating shorter ones into your answer.
■ Making specific points, reducing the general 'waffle' (!)
■ Relating the poems to T's life/Victorian era.

Thanks to Pam Fisher

Doing it yourself

The chapters of this book sample only some of the ways of reading texts. Some of the more theoretically challenging approaches have been left out. You can also make up your own approaches and you will often find that individual poems suggest these alternative ways of reading. Basically, you can read from the point of view of any **context** that you can put the poem into. Here are some examples of further ways of reading:

- What does a series of poems suggest about the natural environment or the built environment? A kind of environmental reading.
- A 'youthist' perspective. Read a set of poems from the perspective of the young, representing their ways of seeing the world.
- The movement that the poet or the poem belongs to. Here you need to compare your informed personal response with the characteristics of that movement, e.g. Metaphysical poetry or the Romantics.
- A 'slow motion' reading showing what expectations are built up in the reader as the poem progresses. Revealing a poem word by word can reveal a great deal about vocabulary and grammar that might have remained invisible.

ACTIVITY 110

Key Skills – these activities can be developed to address several key skills

The critic, Harold Bloom, believes that poetry can offer 'self help'. For example, Queen Victoria was said to have been greatly comforted by Tennyson's *Be near me when my light is low* when her husband, Albert, died in 1861. Using a selection of the poems you have studied, explore this view. You might consider what kinds of lessons the poet might be trying to teach, if any, examining the range of emotions and opinions communicated by the poems.

ACTIVITY 111

Elizabeth Barrett Browning's poetry can be interpreted biographically or from a feminist perspective. Referring to about six poems, prepare and write an essay comparing these two points of view.

ACTIVITY 112

The conquering of new territory can often be an important metaphor in poetry. Compare the ways in which this idea is used in the poetry of John Donne (see page 80) and in the work of some Caribbean poets such as Grace Nichols (see page 47).

ACTIVITY 113

Keats' *La Belle Dame sans Merci* (page 65) can be read as a poem about:

- consumption (or tuberculosis) – which killed Keats, aged 25
- Fanny Brawne – Keats' unrequited love
- The relationship between men and women
- What the goddess of poetry does to her poets.

Return to the poem, testing each of these ways of reading against your own. You may also wish to do some background research. Which reading, if any, do you find most satisfying?

ACTIVITY 114

D. H. Lawrence's poem *After the Opera* (page 46) can be interpreted in terms of

a feminism

or

b social class.

Re-read the poem and build up evidence for both of these readings. Then decide which one you find the most satisfying.

W. H. Auden's *Funeral Blues* (better known as *Song* or *Stop All the Clocks*) appeared in the film *Four Weddings and a Funeral* where it was used as a lament for the death of a character's homosexual lover. This apparently was not Auden's intention. The issue has been discussed in the *Secondary English Magazine*, Vol 3, No 1 and Vol 3, No 4. Using these resources, discuss the interpretation of this poem considering both the author's intention and the new context in which the poem was presented.

Further Reading

Harold Bloom, *How to Read and Why*, Fourth Estate, 2000. This is demanding for students but it does providing a lightning tour of English Literature and is the kind of text that examiners will get their questions from.

Martin Stephen, *English Literature: a Student Guide*, Pearson Education, 2000. A literary history with worked examples and different critical perspectives.

York Notes Advanced, Longman. These now contain sections on various critical approaches.

Websites

There is plenty of useful material out there but it can take forever to find it. Here are two magazine articles designed to save you time:

'The Internet for English Students', in the *English Review*, Vol 10, No 1, Sept 1999.

'ICT 4 English' (aimed at teachers), in the *Secondary English Magazine*, Vol 3, No 2, Nov 1999.